OCS Report
MMS 96-0061

Outer ContinentalShelf

Estimated Proved and Unproved Oil and Gas Reserves, Gulf of Mexico, December 31, 1995

Suzan M. Bacigalupi
Clark J. Kinler
David A. Marin
Michael T. Prendergast

Resource Evaluation Office
Reserves Section

U.S. Department of the Interior
Minerals Management Service
Gulf of Mexico OCS Regional Office

New Orleans
October 1996

Contents

Abstract

Remaining proved reserves in the Gulf of Mexico Outer Continental Shelf (OCS) as of December 31, 1995, have been estimated to be 2.33 billion barrels of oil[1] and 27.5 trillion cubic feet of gas. These reserves are recoverable from 754 proved active fields. Unproved reserves as of December 31, 1995, have been estimated to be 1.20 billion barrels of oil and 4.1 trillion cubic feet of gas. These reserves are associated with 76 unproved active fields. This makes a total of 830 active fields located in Federal waters.

Original proved reserves are estimated to have been 12.01 billion barrels of oil and 144.9 trillion cubic feet of gas from 899 proved fields in the same geographic area. Included in this number are 145 fields that are depleted and abandoned; not included are the 76 unproved active fields. Estimates were made for individual reservoirs based on geologic mapping and reserve evaluation.

The unproved reserves, associated with the 76 unproved active fields, are not added to proved reserves because of different levels of economic certainty and hydrocarbon assurance. For any field contained partly in State waters and partly in Federal waters, reserves are estimated for the Federal portion only.

---

[1] The term "oil" as used in this report includes crude oil and condensate.

Introduction

This report, which supersedes the Minerals Management Service (MMS) OCS Report MMS 95-0050 (Melancon and others, 1995), presents original proved reserves, cumulative production, remaining proved reserves, and unproved reserves as of December 31, 1995, for the Gulf of Mexico (GOM). This report does not consider the reserves growth phenomena when addressing remaining proved reserves. A discussion of reserves growth can be found in OCS Report MMS 96-0047 (Lore and others, 1996). The estimates of reserves for this report were completed in May 1996 and represent the combined efforts of engineers, geologists, geophysicists, paleontologists, and other personnel of the MMS Gulf of Mexico Region, Office of Resource Evaluation, in New Orleans, Louisiana.

As in previous reports, standard methods of estimating reserves were used, including volumetric calculation and performance analyses.

Definition of Resource and Reserve Terms

The MMS definitions and classification schema concerning reserves reflect those of the Society of Petroleum Engineers (SPE) and the World Petroleum Congress (WPC), 1996. SPE definitions have been used since 1988. The MMS definitions and classification schema concerning resources are modified as referenced by the U.S. Department of the Interior (DOI), 1989. The MMS petroleum resource and reserve classifications are represented in figures 1 and 2.

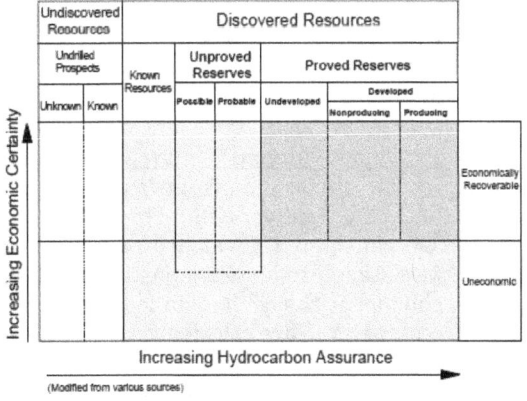

Figure 1.—MMS conventionally recoverable petroleum resource classifications.

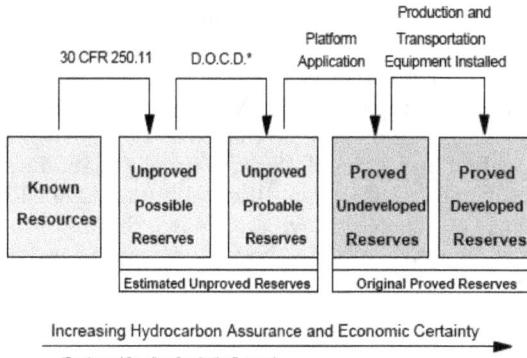

Figure 2.—Gulf of Mexico MMS reserve classifications.

Field
A field is an area consisting of a single reservoir or multiple reservoirs all grouped on, or related to, the same general geological structural feature and/or stratigraphic trapping condition. There may be two or more reservoirs in a field that are separated vertically by intervening impervious strata, or laterally by geological barriers, or both. The area may include one OCS lease, a portion of an OCS lease, or a group of OCS leases with one or more wells that have been approved as producible by the MMS pursuant to the requirements of Title 30 Code of Federal Regulations (CFR) 250.11, Determination of Well Producibility. A field is usually named after the area and block on which the discovery well is located. Field names or field boundaries may be changed when additional geologic and/or production data support such a change. Using geological criteria, the MMS designates a new producible lease as a new field or assigns it to a preexisting field. A further explanation of field naming convention can be found on page 5, and in the *Field Naming Handbook* available on the MMS Gulf of Mexico Region's Internet Homepage at http://www.mms.gov.omm/gomr/.

Undiscovered Resources
Hydrocarbons estimated on the basis of geologic knowledge and theory to exist outside of known accumulations are *undiscovered resources*. Undiscovered resources can exist in prospects (unleased acreage and undrilled leased acreage) or in known fields (undrilled reservoirs).

Discovered Resources
Hydrocarbons whose location and quantity are known or estimated from specific geologic evidence are *discovered resources*. Discovered resources

include known resources, unproved reserves, and proved reserves depending upon economic, technical, contractual, or regulatory criteria.

Known Resources

Hydrocarbons associated with reservoirs penetrated by one or more wells that are not currently qualified under the MMS regulations as capable of producing in paying quantities pursuant to 30 CFR 250.11 are *known resources*. Known resources can exist on active, relinquished, or expired leases and fields.

Reserves

Those quantities of hydrocarbons which are anticipated to be recovered from known accumulations from a given date forward are *reserves*. All reserve estimates involve some degree of uncertainty. The uncertainty depends chiefly on the amount of reliable geologic and engineering data available at the time of the estimate and the interpretation of these data. The relative degree of uncertainty may be conveyed by placing reserves into one of two principal classifications, either unproved or proved.

Unproved Reserves

Those quantities of hydrocarbons which can be estimated with some certainty to be potentially recoverable from known reservoirs, assuming future economic conditions and technological developments, are *unproved reserves*. The MMS Gulf of Mexico Regional Field Names Committee designates a new producible lease as a new field or assigns it to a preexisting field. The reserves associated with new producible leases qualified pursuant to 30 CFR 250.11 are initially considered unproved reserves. Unproved reserves are less certain to be recovered than proved reserves and may be further subclassified as possible and probable reserves to denote progressively increasing certainty in their recoverability. This report does not present individual estimates for possible and probable reserves.

Unproved possible reserves are those unproved reserves which analysis of geological and engineering data suggests are less likely to be commercially recoverable than probable reserves. After a well on a lease qualifies, the reserves associated with the lease are initially classified as unproved possible because the only direct evidence of economic accumulations is a production test or electric log analysis.

Unproved probable reserves are those unproved reserves which analysis of geological and engineering data suggests are more likely than not to be commercially recoverable. Fields that have a Development Operations Coordination Document (DOCD) on file with the MMS would be classified as unproved probable.

Proved Reserves

Those quantities of hydrocarbons which can be estimated with reasonable certainty to be commercially recoverable from known reservoirs and under current economic conditions, operating methods, and government regulations are *proved* reserves. Establishment of current economic conditions includes consideration of relevant historical petroleum prices and associated costs and may involve an averaging period that is consistent with the purpose of the reserve estimate. Proved reserves must have either facilities operational at the time of the estimate to process and transport those reserves to market, or a commitment or reasonable expectation to install such facilities in the future. The application for a permit to install a platform is considered such a commitment. Proved reserves can be subdivided into undeveloped or developed.

Proved undeveloped reserves exist where there is a relatively large expenditure required to install production and/or transportation facilities and a commitment has been made by the operator to develop the field. Proved undeveloped reserves are reserves expected to be recovered from yet undrilled wells or from existing wells where a relatively large expenditure is required for field development.

Proved developed reserves are expected to be recovered from existing wells (including reserves behind pipe). Reserves are considered developed only after the necessary production and transportation equipment has been installed, or when the costs to do so are relatively minor. Proved developed reserves are subcategorized as producing or nonproducing. This distinction is made at the reservoir level.

PROVED DEVELOPED PRODUCING reserves are in reservoirs that have produced any time during the 12 months before the reporting date.

Once the first reservoir in a field begins production, the reservoir and the field are considered proved developed producing.

PROVED DEVELOPED NONPRODUCING reserves are in reservoirs that have not produced during the 12 months prior to the reporting date. This category includes off-production reservoirs behind pipe and reservoirs awaiting workovers or transportation facilities. If all reservoirs in a field are off production, the field is considered proved developed nonproducing.

Reference Standard Conditions for Production and Reserves

Production data are the metered volumes of raw liquids and gas reported to the MMS by Federal unit and lease operators. Oil volume measurements and reserves are corrected to reference standard conditions of 60°F and one atmosphere (14.696 pounds per square inch absolute [psia]); gas measurements and reserves are corrected to 60°F and 15.025 psia. To convert gas volumes to 14.696 psia, multiply by 1.022 (DOE, 1989). Continuously measured volumes from production platforms and/or leases are allocated to individual wells and reservoirs based on periodic well test gauges. These procedures introduce approximations in both production and reserves data.

MMS Reporting of Reserve and Resource Data

OCS reserve estimates have been published by the Gulf of Mexico Region annually since 1977, presenting end of year totals starting with 1975. From 1977 to 1981 the estimates were published as United States Geological Survey (USGS) Open-File reports. The 1982 report was a joint publication between the USGS and the newly formed MMS, which assumed the OCS mission responsibilities at that time. The MMS has continued the reporting since 1983. This is the first report provided by the MMS that also includes unproved reserve estimates.

Figure 3 shows the relationship of evaluated data to hydrocarbon assurance. The data are progressively aggregated on both a geologic and a geographic basis at each step of the evaluation process (the reservoir level through the region level). The most

detailed studies of discovered resources are MMS individual field studies. These studies are based on analysis at the reservoir level (an example being a single fault trap in a single sand) and are used as the basis for the reporting of discovered and undiscovered resources. The geologic aggregation begins at the top of the figure at the reservoir level and progresses downward through the sand, pool, play, chronozone, series, and system to the regional level. Reservoirs correlated to a specific sand are aggregated to form the sand reporting level which becomes the basis for further aggregations of data. A play is defined primarily (though not exclusively) by depositional style, geologic age at the chronozone level, and geographic area. Pools are based on the same characteristics of a play, but are specific to an individual field. Fields may contain one or more pools, with each pool representing a separate play. The geographic aggregation begins at the bottom of the figure, also at the reservoir level, and progresses upward through the field, area, and planning area to the regional level.

This report, *Estimated Proved and Unproved Oil and Gas Reserves*, presents reserve data from the field level up to the series level. This report is based on aggregation of MMS internal field studies completed at the reservoir and sand level. All of the reservoir level data have been linked to the

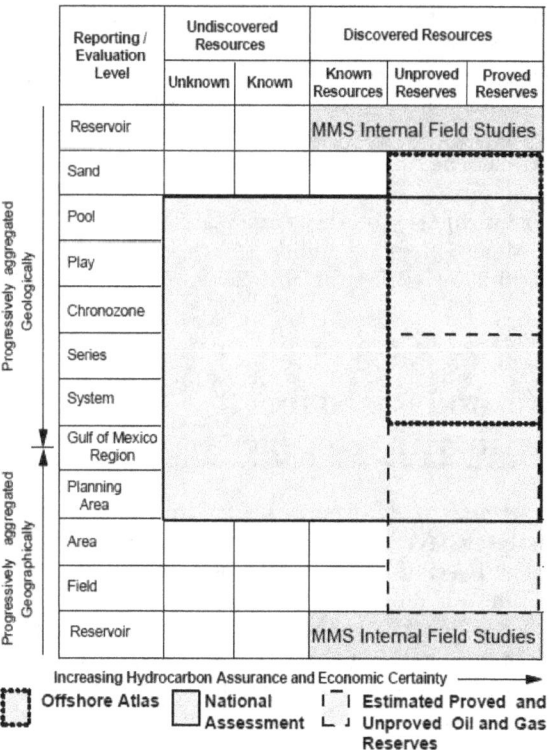

Figure 3.—MMS reporting of reserves and resources.

3

sand, pool, play, chronozone, and series level to support the Offshore Atlas Project (OAP).

A detailed geologic reporting of oil and gas proved reserves, the *Atlas of Northern Gulf of Mexico Gas and Oil Reservoirs, Volume 1: Miocene and Older Reservoirs*, will be available for public release in early 1997. *Volume 2: Plio-Plesitocene Reservoirs* is scheduled for release in mid 1997. Reserve data on every productive sand, as of December 1994, have been placed into 72 proved geological plays in Federal waters. This will be the first MMS release of such a comprehensive framework of geologic and reserve data and the associated attributes for each specific chronozone, play, pool, and sand. Series and system levels can also be evaluated with the data provided. A free abbreviated version of the OAP (pool level data) is available on the GOM Region's Internet Homepage.

The MMS *Summary of the 1995 Assessment of Conventionally Recoverable Hydrocarbon Resources of the Gulf of Mexico and Atlantic Outer Continental Shelf*, also known as the National Assessment, addresses undiscovered resources. To maintain credibility, an estimate of undiscovered resources must be based on discovered resources. The OAP supported this report by providing a framework of hydrocarbon plays which allowed for the logical extension of existing production rather than just a conceptual estimate. This summary report, made available in August 1996, contains resource estimates at the chronozone, series, system, and province (era) levels by planning area, water depth, and region. A more detailed report with resource estimates at the play level will be released in 1997.

For information on these reports, contact the Gulf of Mexico Region's Public Information Office at 1-800-200-GULF or 504-736-2519.

Methods Used for Estimating Reserves

Reserve estimates from geological and engineering analyses have been completed for the 899 proved fields. Reserves accountability is dependent on the drilling and development phases of fields. When a field is in the unproved category, geophysical mapping and limited well data are the basis for defining reservoir limits. Once a field is moved into the proved category and more data become available, the reserve estimate is re-evaluated. Well logs, well file data, seismic data, and

production data are continuously analyzed to improve the accuracy of the reserve estimate. As a field is depleted and abandoned the original proved reserves are assigned a value equal to the amount produced. Currently, there are 145 depleted and abandoned fields.

Estimation of reserves is done under conditions of uncertainty. The method of estimation is called *deterministic* if the estimate is a single "best estimate" based on known geological, engineering, and economic data, and *probabilistic* when the known geologic, engineering, and economic data are analyzed statistically and the estimate determined from continuous probability distributions (SPE/WPC, 1996). Reserve estimates in this report are deterministic.

Reserve estimating methods can be categorized into three (3) groups: analog, volumetric, and performance methods. The accuracy of the original proved reserve estimate improves as more reservoir data become available to geoscientists and engineers. Resources are based on analogy from similar fields, reservoirs, or wells in the same area. Reserve estimates in this report are based primarily on volumetric and performance methods.

Analog

In the estimation of resources by analogy, geoscientists use seismic data to generate pictures of the size and shape of subsurface formations. Before any wells have been drilled on a prospect, estimates of undiscovered resources are based on analogy from similar fields, reservoirs, or wells in the same area. The seismic data help geoscientists identify prospects, but do not provide enough direct data to estimate resources. The effective pore space, water saturation, net hydrocarbon thickness, pressure, volume, and temperature data, necessary to complete resource estimates for prospects, come from nearby field and reservoir well data. After one or more wells are drilled and found productive, a volumetric estimate is done. Resource estimates are not included in this report.

Volumetric

In a volumetric reserve estimate, data from drilled wells and seismic surveys are used to develop geologic interpretations. The effective pore space (porosity), water saturation, and net hydrocarbon thickness of the subsurface formations are calculated through evaluation of well logs, core analysis, and formation test data. Subsurface formations are mapped to determine area and net hydrocarbon thickness for each reservoir. Reservoir pressure, fluid volume, and temperature data from formation fluid samples are used to determine the change in volume of oil and gas as it flows from higher pressure deep underground to lower pressure at the surface. All of these data are compiled, analyzed and applied to standard equations for the calculation of hydrocarbons in-place within the reservoirs. Standard recovery factor equations are then applied to the hydrocarbon in-place estimates to calculate original proved and unproved reserves.

Performance Methods

In performance-technique methods, reserves are estimated using mathematical or graphical techniques of production decline curve analysis and material balance. These techniques are used throughout the oil industry in assessing individual well, reservoir, or field performance and in forecasting future reserves. In decline analysis, a plot of daily production rate against time is most frequently used. Once a well or reservoir can no longer produce at its maximum capacity, the production rate declines. This production rate plotted against time can be extrapolated into the future to predict the remaining reserves. Another type of decline analysis is daily production rate plotted against cumulative oil production, which can also be used to predict remaining reserves. The declining daily rate is extrapolated to predict remaining reserves.

Another performance method, material balance, is used to estimate the amount of hydrocarbons in place. Given the premise that the pressure-volume relationship of a reservoir remains constant as hydrocarbons are produced, it is possible to equate expansion of reservoir fluids with reservoir voidage caused by fluid withdrawal minus any water influx. For depletion-drive gas reservoirs, a plot of pressure/gas compressibility factor (P/Z) versus cumulative gas production gives a good estimate of original gas-in-place. Original recoverable gas reserves are extrapolated to an abandonment reservoir pressure.

Reserves and Related Data Reported by Area

The Gulf of Mexico has been divided into three planning areas for administrative purposes; these planning areas (Western, Central, and Eastern) are shown in figures 4, 5, and 6, respectively. Each planning area is subdivided into smaller areas, which in turn are divided into numbered blocks. Fields in the Gulf of Mexico are identified by the

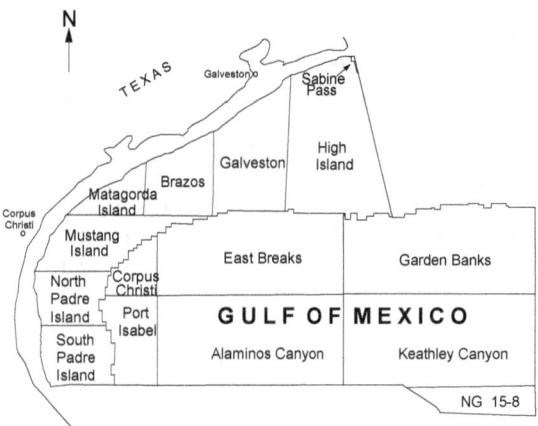

Figure 4.—Western Planning Area, Gulf of Mexico, Outer Continental Shelf.

Figure 5.—Central Planning Area, Gulf of Mexico, Outer Continental Shelf.

Figure 6.—Eastern Planning Area, Gulf of Mexico, Outer Continental Shelf.

smaller area name and block number of discovery — for example, East Cameron Block 271 Field. As the field is developed, the limits often expand into adjacent blocks and areas. These adjacent blocks are then identified as part of the original field and are given that field name. Statistics in this report are presented as area totals compiled under each field name. All of the data associated with East Cameron Block 271 Field are therefore included in the East Cameron totals, although part of the field extends into the adjacent area of Vermilion. There are four exceptions to the above field-naming techniques: Tiger Shoal and Lighthouse Point, included in South Marsh Island; Coon Point, included in Ship Shoal; and Bay Marchand, included in South Timbalier.

There were 830 active fields in the federally regulated part of the Gulf of Mexico, as listed in the *Field Names Master List (April 1996)*.

An updated list can be found on the MMS GOM Region's Internet Homepage. For this report, 754 proved active fields and 76 unproved active fields were studied. Also included were 145 proved depleted fields (abandoned with production) to give a complete record of cumulative oil and gas production. Not studied were 136 fields expired, relinquished, or terminated without production. In 1995 thirteen proved fields were depleted and 6 unproved fields expired.

Reserves data and various classifications of fields, leases, boreholes, and completions are presented as area totals in tables 1 and 2, and the table 3 series. Dashes on these tables are used to preserve the proprietary nature of data. (The table 3 series will be discussed in the section "Reserves Reported by Geologic Age," beginning on page 8.)

Table 1.—Estimated oil and gas reserves for 899 proved and 76 unproved fields by area, Gulf of Mexico, Outer Continental Shelf, December 31, 1995.

(Reserves: oil expressed in millions of barrels at 60°F and 1 atmosphere, gas in billions of cubic feet at 60°F

Area(s) (Figs. 4, 5, and 6)	Number of fields					Original proved reserves		Cumulative production through 1995		Remaining proved reserves		Estimated unproved reserves	
	Proved active prod	Proved active nonprod	Proved expired depleted	Unproved active	Expired nonprod	Oil	Gas	Oil	Gas	Oil	Gas	Oil	Gas
Western Planning Area													
Brazos	31	1	5	0	3	11	3,046	8	2,251	3	795	-	-
Galveston	23	1	16	1	5	38	1,583	28	1,304	10	279	-	-
High Island and Sabine Pass	87	0	24	4	17	344	12,858	263	10,953	81	1,905	-	-
Matagorda Island	29	0	0	1	2	22	4,850	15	3,372	7	1,478	-	-
Mustang Island	20	2	4	0	6	8	2,029	4	1,081	4	948	-	-
N. & S. Padre Island	7	0	1	0	2	1	507	0	361	1	146	-	-
Western Slope*	10	0	0	11	10	214	1,637	78	698	136	939	-	-
Western Planning Area Subtotal	*207*	*4*	*50*	*17*	*45*	*638*	*26,510*	*396*	*20,020*	*242*	*6,490*	*219*	*1,350*
Central Planning Area													
Chandeleur	8	0	1	0	0	0	371	0	276	0	95	-	-
East Cameron	42	0	15	1	5	296	9,563	242	8,433	54	1,130	-	-
Eugene Island	59	1	8	2	6	1,472	17,192	1,234	14,648	238	2,544	-	-
Grand Isle	11	0	3	1	2	922	4,070	843	3,661	79	409	-	-
Main Pass and Breton Sound	45	0	8	3	10	964	5,113	765	4,041	199	1,072	-	-
Mobile	18	4	0	0	4	0	2,172	0	438	0	1,734	-	-
Ship Shoal	49	0	9	3	7	1,226	10,964	1,083	9,639	143	1,325	-	-
South Marsh Island	41	1	5	2	4	788	13,259	695	11,417	93	1,842	-	-
South Pass	12	0	0	1	1	1,062	4,049	875	3,046	187	1,003	-	-
South Pelto	7	1	2	0	0	138	810	117	644	21	166	-	-
South Timbalier	34	2	5	3	9	1,317	7,447	1,204	6,301	113	1,146	-	-
Vermilion	66	2	8	3	7	477	15,287	407	13,448	70	1,839	-	-
Viosca Knoll	10	3	0	4	0	0	188	0	54	0	134	-	-
West Cameron and Sabine Pass	74	3	25	2	8	169	17,304	141	14,966	28	2,338	-	-
West Delta	18	0	4	1	2	1,297	4,798	1,175	4,244	122	554	-	-
Central Slope†	28	4	2	29	25	1,246	5,852	506	2,137	740	3,715	-	-
Central Planning Area Subtotal	*522*	*21*	*95*	*55*	*90*	*11,374*	*118,439*	*9,287*	*97,393*	*2,087*	*21,046*	*982*	*2,769*
Eastern Planning Area Subtotal‡	*0*	*0*	*0*	*4*	*1*	*-*	*-*	*-*	*-*	*-*	*-*	*-*	*-*
GOM Total	*729*	*25*	*145* / *899*	*76*	*136*	*12,012*	*144,949*	*9,683*	*117,413*	*2,329*	*27,536*	*1,201*	*4,119*

*Western Slope includes Alaminos Canyon, Corpus Christi, East Breaks, Garden Banks, Keathley Canyon, and Port Isabel.
†Central Slope includes Atwater Valley, Ewing Bank, Green Canyon, Lund, Mississippi Canyon, Viosca Knoll (slope), and Walker Ridge.
‡Eastern Planning Area includes Charlotte Harbor, Destin Dome, Pensacola and others. Unproved reserves data are included with Central Planning Area.

Figure 7 provides a geographical representation of locations for the 899 proved fields in the Gulf of Mexico. Estimates of proved reserves for these fields, both producing and nonproducing, are presented as area totals in table 1. Figure 8 provides a geographical representation of the 76 unproved active fields in the Gulf of Mexico. Estimates of unproved reserves are presented as planning area subtotals. The Eastern Planning Area totals for unproved reserves are included in the Central Planning Area subtotals.

The status of Gulf of Mexico OCS Federal oil and gas leases as of December 31, 1995, is represented in table 2. There are 5,068 active leases (1,833 proved active, 98 unproved qualified, and 3,137 unproved active) and 7,685 relinquished leases (587 proved depleted and 7,098 expired).

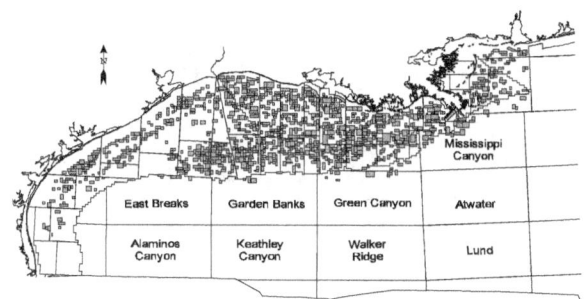

Figure 7.—Gulf of Mexico, 899 proved fields (754 active and 145 depleted).

Table 2.—Status of oil and gas leases, boreholes, and completions by area, Gulf of Mexico, Outer Continental Shelf, December 31, 1995.

(All statistics associated with fields are presented within area totals compiled under each field name.)

Area(s) (Figs. 4, 5, and 6)	Number of leases					Number of boreholes		Number of active completions
	Proved active	Proved depleted	Unproved qualified	Unproved active	Expired	Drilled	Abandoned	
Western Planning Area								
Brazos	56	12	0	69	212	455	277	194
Galveston	44	26	2	83	418	537	413	149
High Island and Sabine Pass	169	65	3	173	689	2,414	1,372	1,101
Matagorda Island	64	8	1	23	109	496	210	326
Mustang Island	40	4	0	48	304	337	198	156
N. & S. Padre Island	11	3	0	31	230	133	91	54
Western Slope*	25	2	16	466	707	403	241	125
Western Planning Area Subtotal	*409*	*120*	*22*	*893*	*2,669*	*4,775*	*2,802*	*2,105*
Central Planning Area								
Chandeleur	12	2	0	4	23	62	30	32
East Cameron	101	54	1	138	376	1,608	1,008	703
Eugene Island	190	53	2	97	323	3,827	2,025	1,888
Grand Isle	48	8	1	35	96	1,283	823	617
Main Pass and Breton Sound	118	34	4	106	253	1,921	820	1,367
Mobile	34	0	0	26	49	94	39	49
Ship Shoal	153	37	3	98	323	2,982	1,631	1,507
South Marsh Island	99	31	2	72	205	2,191	1,083	1,133
South Pass	50	5	1	18	63	1,884	916	1,029
South Pelto	16	3	0	8	22	331	196	152
South Timbalier	109	24	6	99	309	2,483	1,198	1,507
Vermilion	156	65	6	137	373	2,425	1,389	1,067
Viosca Knoll	17	0	6	65	86	58	22	21
West Cameron and Sabine Pass	180	124	1	218	554	2,712	1,731	1,059
West Delta	62	23	1	34	130	2,071	1,225	1,027
Central Slope†	79	4	37	937	917	1,299	785	451
Central Planning Area Subtotal	*1,424*	*467*	*71*	*2,092*	*4,102*	*27,321*	*14,921*	*13,669*
Eastern Planning Area Subtotal‡	*0*	*0*	*5*	*152*	*327*	*46*	*40*	*0*
GOM Total	*1,833*	*587*	*98*	*3,137*	*7,098*	*32,142*	*17,763*	*15,774*

*Western Slope includes Alaminos Canyon, Corpus Christi, East Breaks, Garden Banks, Keathley Canyon, and Port Isabel.
†Central Slope includes Atwater Valley, Ewing Bank, Green Canyon, Lund, Mississippi Canyon, Viosca Knoll (slope), and Walker Ridge.
‡Eastern Planning Area includes Charlotte Harbor, Destin Dome, Pensacola and others. Unproved reserves data are included with Central Planning Area.

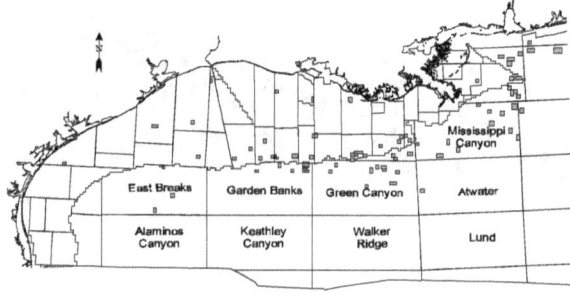

Figure 8.—Gulf of Mexico, 76 unproved active fields.

Definitions of the table 2 subgroups follow:

Proved Active — Leases within the designated 754 proved active fields presented in table 1.

Proved Depleted — Leases relinquished after oil and gas production. The leases associated with the 145 depleted fields are represented here along with other produced, relinquished leases that are part of currently active fields.

Unproved Qualified — Leases associated with the 76 unproved active fields. The leases have qualified as producible under 30 CFR 250.11, but the operators have not established a commitment to produce. These fields may be classified as unproved possible or unproved probable.

Unproved Active — Active exploratory leases not yet qualified as producible or associated with any field.

Expired — Leases relinquished by the operator without having produced any oil or gas, although some were once qualified as producible under 30 CFR 250.11. There are 136 expired fields with no production.

The total number of boreholes drilled and the number of boreholes plugged and abandoned are also shown in table 2. There were 905 boreholes spudded during 1995, compared with 907 during 1994 and 808 during 1993. The last column of table 2 presents the total number of active completions per area. Active completions are defined as those with perforations open to the formation and not isolated by permanent plugs; service wells (injection, disposal, or water source) are included. The presence or absence of production or injection is not considered. The number of boreholes and the number of active completions as of December 31, 1995, are based on reports received by the MMS at the time the count was made in 1996. These numbers may change when all data have been received, processed, and edited.

Reserves Reported by Geologic Age

In this report the 899 proved and 76 unproved fields have been classified at the geologic series level. The different geologic age classifications in use by MMS are shown in figure 9. Paleontological examinations of borehole cuttings, along with regional analysis of geological and geophysical data, were used in determining the age classifications. Table 3 shows the distribution of reserves and production data by geologic age and planning area. Tables 3a through 3d also show the distribution of reserves and production data by geologic age, but further subdivide the planning areas as area totals. Unproved reserves are not reported as area totals to maintain the confidential nature of unproved fields.

Era or Erathem	Period or System	Epoch or Series	Chronozones (Used in Reporting Resources)	Informal Geologic Times M.Y.A.*	Biozones
	Quaternary	Holocene		0.01	Trimosina "A" / Hyalinea "B"
		Pleistocene	UPL		Angulogerina "B"
			MPL		Lenticulina 1 / Valvulineria "H"
			LPL	2.8	
		Pliocene	UP		Buliminella 1
			LP	5.5	Textularia "X"
	Neogene		UM 3		Robulus "E" / Bigenerina "A" / Cristellaria "K"
			UM 1		Discorbis 12 / Textularia "L"
			MM 9	10.5	Bigenerina 2 / Textularia "W"
Cenozoic		Miocene	MM 7		Bigenerina humblei / Cristellaria "I" / Cibicides opima
	Tertiary		MM 4		Amphistegina "B" / Gyroidina "K"
			LM 4	18.5	Discorbis "B" / Marginulina "A"
			LM 2		Siphonia davisi
			LM 1		Lenticulina hanseni / Cristellaria "R"
		Oligocene	O	24.8	Discorbis zone
	Paleogene	Eocene	E	38	
		Paleocene	L	55	
	Cretaceous		K	63	
Mesozoic	Jurassic		U	138	
	Triassic		TR	205 ~240	

(Modified from various published and unpublished sources) * Million Years Anum

Figure 9.—Gulf of Mexico MMS geologic time scale.

Table 3.—Estimated oil and gas reserves for 899 proved and 76 unproved fields by geologic age, Gulf of Mexico, Outer Continental Shelf, December 31, 1995.

(Reserves: oil expressed in millions of barrels at 60°F and 1 atmosphere, gas in billions of cubic feet at 60°F and 15.025 psia.)

Geologic Age	Number of proved reservoirs	Original proved reserves		Cumulative production through 1995		Remaining proved reserves		Number of unproved reservoirs	Estimated unproved reserves	
		Oil	Gas	Oil	Gas	Oil	Gas		Oil	Gas
Western Planning Area										
Pleistocene	1,383	469	10,520	285	8,365	184	2,155	78	166	1,072
Pliocene	4	52	118	25	56	27	62	10	53	271
Miocene	1,974	117	15,838	86	11,599	31	4,239	5	0	7
Oligocene, Cretaceous, and Jurassic	8	0	34	0	0	0	34	0	0	0
Western Planning Area Subtotal	*3,369*	*638*	*26,510*	*396*	*20,020*	*242*	*6,490*	*93*	*219*	*1,350*
Central Planning Area										
Pleistocene	7,835	3,842	47,596	3,133	39,645	709	7,951	102	226	763
Pliocene	5,726	3,475	22,362	2,850	18,236	625	4,126	43	213	286
Miocene	5,905	4,057	46,648	3,304	39,216	753	7,432	53	542	1,125
Oligocene, Cretaceous, and Jurassic	15	0	1,833	0	296	0	1,537	2	1	595
Central Planning Area Subtotal	*19,481*	*11,374*	*118,439*	*9,287*	*97,393*	*2,087*	*21,046*	*200*	*982*	*2,769*
Eastern Planning Area Subtotal‡	*0*	*0*	*0*	*0*	*0*	*0*	*0*	*0*	*0*	*0*
GOM Total	*22,850*	*12,012*	*144,949*	*9,683*	*117,413*	*2,329*	*27,536*	*293*	*1,201*	*4,119*

‡Eastern Planning Area includes Charlotte Harbor, Destin Dome, Pensacola and others. Unproved data are included with Central Planning Area.

Table 3a.—Estimated oil and gas reserves for Pleistocene reservoirs in 469 proved and 33 unproved fields by area, Gulf of Mexico, Outer Continental Shelf, December 31, 1995.

(Reserves: oil expressed in millions of barrels at 60°F and 1 atmosphere, gas in billions of cubic feet at 60°F and 15.025 psia.)

Area(s)	Number of proved reservoirs	Original proved reserves		Cumulative production through 1995		Remaining proved reserves		Number of unproved reservoirs	Estimated unproved reserves	
		Oil	Gas	Oil	Gas	Oil	Gas		Oil	Gas
Western Planning Area										
Galveston	25	1	82	0	65	1	17	0	-	-
High Island and Sabine Pass	1,214	306	8,915	232	7,654	74	1,261	12	-	-
Western Slope*	144	162	1,523	53	646	109	877	66	-	-
Western Planning Area Subtotal	*1,383*	*469*	*10,520*	*285*	*8,365*	*184*	*2,155*	*78*	*166*	*1,072*
Central Planning Area										
East Cameron	609	213	4,751	171	4,038	42	713	2	-	-
Eugene Island	1,665	927	11,476	767	9,927	160	1,549	3	-	-
Grand Isle	93	7	1,330	6	1,202	1	128	0	-	-
Main Pass and Breton Sound	20	47	120	29	93	18	27	0	-	-
Ship Shoal	1,385	761	6,624	686	5,920	75	704	3	-	-
South Marsh Island	740	473	3,414	420	2,806	53	608	1	-	-
South Pass	180	161	1,319	122	985	39	334	2	-	-
South Pelto	82	23	21	19	15	4	6	0	-	-
South Timbalier	961	309	4,531	270	3,818	39	713	5	-	-
Vermilion	761	160	3,326	123	2,645	37	681	21	-	-
Viosca Knoll	1	0	0	0	0	0	0	0	-	-
West Cameron and Sabine Pass	779	28	7,332	21	6,209	7	1,123	3	-	-
West Delta	158	186	704	171	573	15	131	0	-	-
Central Slope†	401	547	2,648	328	1,414	219	1,234	62	-	-
Central Planning Area Subtotal	*7,835*	*3,842*	*47,596*	*3,133*	*39,645*	*709*	*7,951*	*102*	*226*	*763*
GOM Total	*9,218*	*4,311*	*58,116*	*3,418*	*48,010*	*893*	*10,106*	*180*	*392*	*1,835*

* Western Slope includes Alaminos Canyon, Corpus Christi, East Breaks, Garden Banks, Keathley Canyon, and Port Isabel.
†Central Slope includes Atwater Valley, Ewing Bank, Green Canyon, Lund, Mississippi Canyon, Viosca Knoll (slope), and Walker Ridge.

9

Table 3b.—Estimated oil and gas reserves for Pliocene reservoirs in 255 proved and 17 unproved fields by area, Gulf of Mexico, Outer Continental Shelf, December 31, 1995.

(Reserves: oil expressed in millions of barrels at 60° F and 1 atmosphere, gas in billions of cubic feet at 60°F and 15.025 psia.)

Area(s)	Number of proved reservoirs	Original proved reserves		Cumulative production through 1995		Remaining proved reserves		Number of unproved reservoirs	Estimated unproved reserves	
		Oil	Gas	Oil	Gas	Oil	Gas		Oil	Gas
Western Planning Area										
High Island and Sabine Pass	2	0	4	0	4	0	0	0	-	-
Western Slope*	2	52	114	25	52	27	62	10	-	-
Western Planning Area Subtotal	*4*	*52*	*118*	*25*	*56*	*27*	*62*	*10*	*53*	*271*
Central Planning Area										
Chandeleur	2	0	13	0	9	0	4	0	-	-
East Cameron	140	12	828	9	669	3	159	0	-	-
Eugene Island	1,025	406	2,567	351	2,028	55	539	0	-	-
Grand Isle	325	357	976	316	852	41	124	5	-	-
Main Pass and Breton Sound	323	175	1,238	119	951	56	287	0	-	-
Ship Shoal	628	307	2,291	268	1,952	39	339	5	-	-
South Marsh Island	564	130	4,226	116	3,790	14	436	0	-	-
South Pass	737	775	2,165	647	1,616	128	549	1	-	-
South Pelto	157	64	236	57	208	7	28	0	-	-
South Timbalier	474	238	1,378	209	1,121	29	257	0	-	-
Vermilion	527	171	3,061	152	2,611	19	450	2	-	-
West Cameron and Sabine Pass	151	2	993	2	803	0	190	0	-	-
West Delta	553	492	1,114	427	916	65	198	0	-	-
Central Slope†	120	346	1,276	177	710	169	566	30	-	-
Central Planning Area Subtotal	*5,726*	*3,475*	*22,362*	*2,850*	*18,236*	*625*	*4,126*	*43*	*213*	*286*
GOM Total	*5,730*	*3,527*	*22,480*	*2,875*	*18,292*	*652*	*4,188*	*53*	*266*	*557*

* Western Slope includes Alaminos Canyon, Corpus Christi, East Breaks, Garden Banks, Keathley Canyon , and Port Isabel.
†Central Slope includes Atwater Valley, Ewing Bank, Green Canyon, Lund, Mississippi Canyon, Viosca Knoll (slope), and Walker Ridge.

The Pleistocene production trend is presented in figure 10 and corresponds to the *Trimosina* "A" through *Valvulineria* "H" biozones. Production within the Pleistocene extends from the Galveston area to east of the modern-day mouth of the Mississippi River. Pleistocene productive sands are limited to the east and west because of a lack of sediment influx at the edge of the depocenter. Downdip deepwater Pleistocene production occurs in the East Breaks through Mississippi Canyon areas, and well control suggests sands continuing beyond the Sigsbee Escarpment. As of December 31, 1995, the Pleistocene produced from 469 fields. Original proved reserves were 4.31 billion barrels (Bbbl) and 58.1 trillion cubic feet (Tcf). Remaining proved reserves were 0.89 Bbbl and 10.1 Tcf.

The Pliocene production trend is presented in figure 11 and corresponds to the *Buliminella* 1 through *Textularia* X biozones. Production within the Pliocene extends from south of Mobile Bay in the east to North Padre Island in the west. Upper

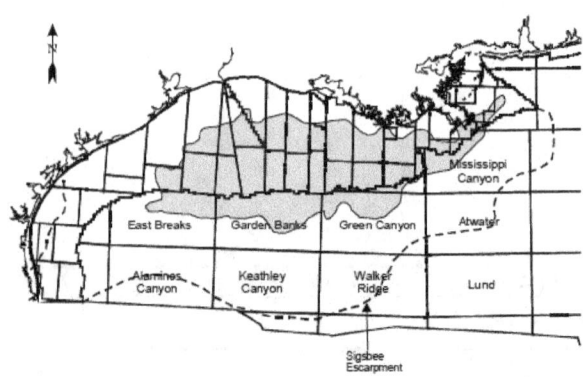

Figure 10.—Pleistocene production trend.

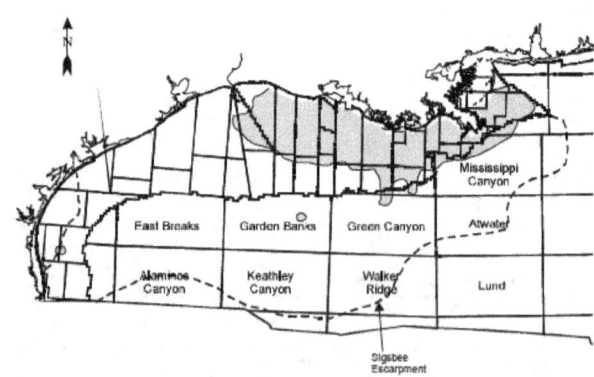

Figure 11.—Pliocene production trend.

Table 3c.—Estimated oil and gas reserves for Miocene reservoirs in 458 proved and 24 unproved fields by area, Gulf of Mexico, Outer Continental Shelf, December 31, 1995.

(Reserves: oil expressed in millions of barrels at 60°F and 1 atmosphere, gas in billions of cubic feet at 60°F and 15.025 psia.)

Area(s)	Number of proved reservoirs	Original proved reserves		Cumulative production through 1995		Remaining proved reserves		Number of unproved reservoirs	Estimated unproved reserves	
		Oil	Gas	Oil	Gas	Oil	Gas		Oil	Gas
Western Planning Area										
Brazos	386	11	3,046	8	2,251	3	795	0	-	-
Galveston	343	37	1,501	28	1,239	9	262	3	-	-
High Island and Sabine Pass	417	38	3,939	31	3,295	7	644	0	-	-
Matagorda Island	416	22	4,850	15	3,372	7	1,478	2	-	-
Mustang Island	329	8	1,995	4	1,081	4	914	0	-	-
N. & S. Padre Island	83	1	507	0	361	1	146	0	-	-
Western Slope*	0	0	0	0	0	0	0	0	-	-
Western Planning Area Subtotal	*1,974*	*117*	*15,838*	*86*	*11,599*	*31*	*4,239*	*5*	*0*	*7*
Central Planning Area										
Chandeleur	22	0	358	0	267	0	91	0	-	-
East Cameron	274	71	3,984	62	3,726	9	258	0	-	-
Eugene Island	404	139	3,149	116	2,693	23	456	1	-	-
Grand Isle	467	558	1,764	521	1,607	37	157	0	-	-
Main Pass and Breton Sound	796	742	3,755	617	2,997	125	758	1	-	-
Mobile	28	0	339	0	142	0	197	0	-	-
Ship Shoal	443	158	2,049	129	1,767	29	282	0	-	-
South Marsh Island	394	185	5,619	159	4,821	26	798	0	-	-
South Pass	211	126	565	106	445	20	120	0	-	-
South Pelto	198	51	553	41	421	10	132	0	-	-
South Timbalier	586	770	1,538	725	1,362	45	176	3	-	-
Vermilion	507	146	8,900	132	8,192	14	708	0	-	-
Viosca Knoll	24	0	188	0	54	0	134	3	-	-
West Cameron and Sabine Pass	945	139	8,979	118	7,954	21	1,025	0	-	-
West Delta	566	619	2,980	577	2,755	42	225	3	-	-
Central Slope†	40	353	1,928	1	13	352	1,915	38	-	-
Central Planning Area Subtotal	*5,905*	*4,057*	*46,648*	*3,304*	*39,216*	*753*	*7,432*	*49*	*542*	*1,125*
Eastern Planning Area Subtotal‡	-	-	-	-	-	-	-	*4*	-	-
GOM Total	**7,879**	**4,174**	**62,486**	**3,390**	**50,815**	**784**	**11,671**	**58**	**542**	**1,132**

*Western Slope includes Alaminos Canyon, Corpus Christi, East Breaks, Garden Banks, Keathley Canyon, and Port Isabel.
†Central Slope includes Atwater Valley, Ewing Bank, Green Canyon, Lund, Mississippi Canyon, Viosca Knoll (slope), and Walker Ridge.
‡Eastern Planning Area includes Charlotte Harbor, Destin Dome, Pensacola and others. Unproved reserve data are included with Central Planning Area.

Table 3d.—Estimated oil and gas reserves for Oligocene, Cretaceous, and Jurassic age reservoirs in 12 proved and 2 unproved fields by area, Gulf of Mexico, Outer Continental Shelf, December 31, 1995.

(Reserves: oil expressed in millions of barrels at 60°F and 1 atmosphere, gas in billions of cubic feet at 60°F and 15.025 psia.)

Area(s)	Number of proved reservoirs	Original proved reserves		Cumulative production through 1995		Remaining proved reserves		Number of unproved reservoirs	Estimated unproved reserves	
		Oil	Gas	Oil	Gas	Oil	Gas		Oil	Gas
Western Planning Area										
Mustang Island	8	0	34	0	0	0	34	0	-	-
Western Planning Area Subtotal	*8*	*0*	*34*	*0*	*0*	*0*	*34*	*0*	*0*	*0*
Central Planning Area										
Mobile	14	0	1,833	0	296	0	1,537	0	-	-
Main Pass and Breton Sound	1	0	0	0	0	0	0	0	-	-
Viosca Knoll	0	0	0	0	0	0	0	1	-	-
Central Planning Area Subtotal	*15*	*0*	*1,833*	*0*	*296*	*0*	*1,537*	*1*	*1*	*595*
Eastern Planning Area Subtotal‡	*0*	*0*	*0*	*0*	*0*	*0*	*0*	*1*	-	-
GOM Total	**23**	**0**	**1,867**	**0**	**296**	**0**	**1,571**	**2**	**1**	**595**

‡Eastern Planning Area includes Charlotte Harbor, Destin Dome, Pensacola and others. Unproved reserve data are included with Central Planning Area.

Pliocene productive sands also extend into the deepwater areas of Garden Banks, Green Canyon, Ewing Bank, and Mississippi Canyon. Well control suggests Pliocene sands extend at least as far as the Sigsbee Escarpment. As of December 31, 1995, the Pliocene produced from 255 fields. Original proved reserves were 3.53 Bbbl and 22.5 Tcf. Remaining proved reserves were 0.65 Bbbl and 4.2 Tcf.

The Miocene production trend is presented in figure 12 and corresponds to the *Robulus* "E"/*Bigenerina* "A" through *Cristellaria* "R" biozones. Production within the Miocene extends from east of the Mississippi River to as far west as North Padre Island. Miocene productive sands also extend into deep waters in Viosca Knoll and Mississippi Canyon. Well control suggests sands continuing beyond the Sigsbee Escarpment. As of December 31, 1995, the Miocene produced from 561 fields. Original proved reserves were 4.17 Bbbl and 62.5 Tcf. Remaining proved reserves were 0.78 Bbbl and 11.7 Tcf.

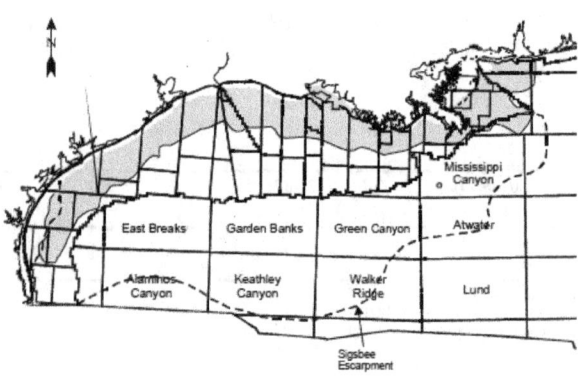

Figure 12.—Miocene production trend.

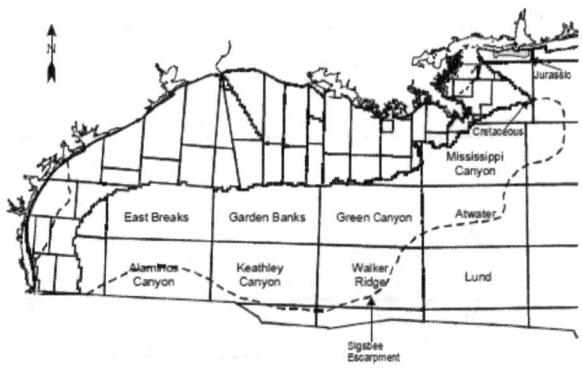

Figure 13.—Oligocene, Cretaceous, and Jurassic production trends.

The Oligocene, Cretaceous, and Jurassic production trends are presented in figure 13. These reservoirs are almost entirely Jurassic Norphlet sands. Production within the Jurassic is limited to east of the Mississippi River in the Mobile area. Well control suggests reservoir sands continuing eastward through Destin Dome; the downdip extension of the Norphlet has yet to be determined. As of December 31, 1995, these trends produced from 12 fields. Original proved reserves were 0 Bbbl and 1.9 Tcf. Remaining proved reserves were 0 Bbbl and 1.57 Tcf.

Figure 14 shows the percentages of reserves and production data by geologic age. There is a fairly even distribution of oil reserves; however, the Pliocene has a significantly lower percentage of gas reserves than the Miocene and Pleistocene.

Age	Original Proved Reserves		Cumulative Production		Remaining Proved Reserves	
	Oil	Gas	Oil	Gas	Oil	Gas
Pleistocene	36 %	40 %	35 %	41 %	38 %	37 %
Pliocene	30 %	16 %	30 %	16 %	29 %	15 %
Miocene	34 %	43 %	35 %	43 %	33 %	42 %
Oligocene, Cretaceous, and Jurassic	–	1 %	–	–	–	6 %

Figure 14.—Distribution of reserves and production data by geologic age.

Historical Exploration and Discovery Pattern and Trends

In large part, the following section was taken from *An Exploration and Discovery Model: a Historic Perspective - Gulf of Mexico Outer Continental Shelf* by Gary Lore. The information presented has been updated to reflect the current database.

It is informative to review the historic exploration and development activities that resulted in the world-class hydrocarbon-producing basin that is the Gulf of Mexico. Each of the four decades of activity will be examined by reviewing the status of exploration and development activity and the number of fields and quantities of proved reserves discovered during each decade. The discovery year is defined as the year in which the first well encountering significant hydrocarbons reached total depth. This date may differ from the year in which the field discovery was announced.

Figure 15 shows the locations of the proved fields discovered prior to December 31, 1959. As expected, initial development was in shallower, nearshore waters concentrated mainly in the areas off central and western Louisiana. This development primarily reflected the gradual extension of existing inland drilling and development technologies into the open-water marine environments, and the infancy of marine seismic acquisition activities. Early exploratory drilling in very shallow water on the shelf utilized barges and platforms. The mid-1950's witnessed the introduction of submersible and jack-up drilling rigs. During this period, 247 exploratory wells were drilled, culminating in the discovery of 68 proved fields. It was also during this period that 7 of the top 10 fields in the Gulf of Mexico, based on original recoverable reserves, were discovered.

Figure 16 shows the location of the proved fields discovered in the 1960's. These discoveries were still concentrated offshore central and western Louisiana. Though still confined to the shelf (600 feet (ft) or less), field discoveries advanced seaward into deeper waters. The introduction of drillships and semisubmersibles for exploratory drilling provided the basis for the deepwater drilling seen today. During this decade, 2,019 exploratory wells were drilled and 134 proved fields discovered. The ninth and tenth largest fields in the Gulf of Mexico, SS 208 and SP 061, were discovered in the sixties.

Figure 17 shows the location of the proved fields discovered in the 1970's. This period reflects continued drilling and development on the shelf, with an increase in field discoveries on the seaward portion of the shelf, predominantly in the Pleistocene depocenter. The introduction of dynamic positioning systems, used on drillships and semi-submersible drilling rigs, further opened up deepwater exploration. Frontier drilling on the shelf-slope margin led to discoveries of new fields that have been termed the *Flexure Trend*. During this decade 2,934 exploratory wells were drilled, resulting in the discovery of 280 proved fields. The largest field in the Gulf of Mexico, EI 330, was discovered in 245 ft of water during this decade. Another significant field discovery was MC 194, the first field in over 1,000 ft of water.

During the 1980's, development activities occurred over practically the entire central and western Gulf

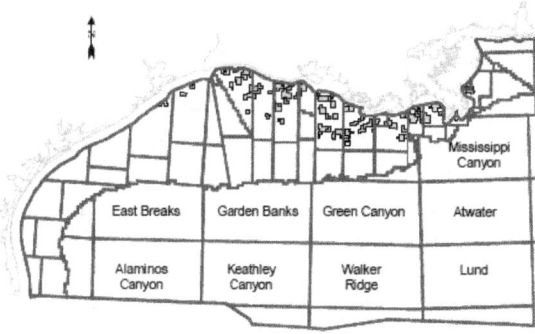

Figure 15.—Location of proved fields discovered 1947-1959, Gulf of Mexico OCS.

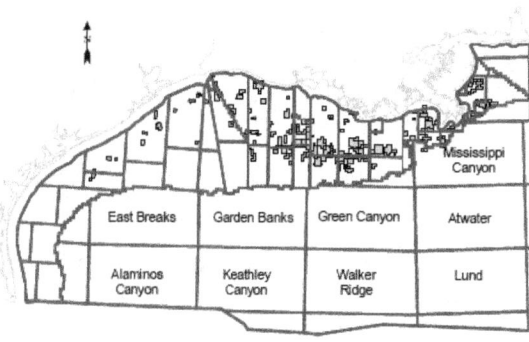

Figure 16.—Location of proved fields discovered 1960-1969, Gulf of Mexico OCS.

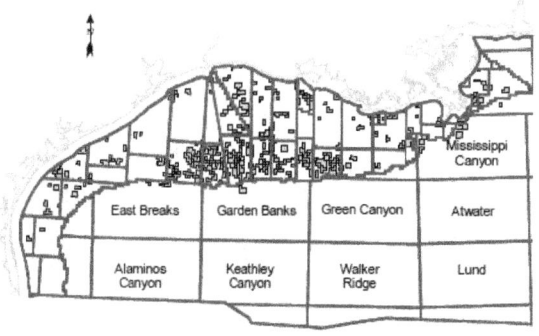

Figure 17.—Location of proved fields discovered 1970-1979, Gulf of Mexico OCS.

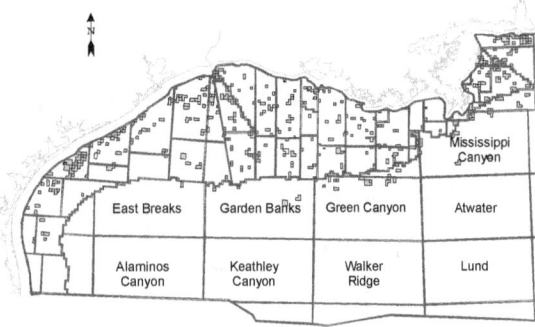

Figure 18.—Location of proved fields discovered 1980-1989, Gulf of Mexico OCS.

of Mexico shelf, as well as on the upper slope, as can be seen in figure 18. In addition, the first Norphlet fields and a Miocene shallow bright spot play were discovered in the eastern Central Gulf of Mexico planning area. Exploratory drilling had now reached water depths beyond 6,000 ft, putting the slope within reach. In this decade, seven proved fields were discovered in water depths greater than 1,000 ft.

From 1990 to 1995 (figure 19), 2,018 exploration wells were drilled, resulting in the discovery of 81 proved fields. The 1990's have seen the refinement and reduction in cost of tension leg platform design, and a much expanded use of subsea completions. Available production histories have documented high production rates for deepwater fields. The expanding use of horizontal drilling is also increasing productivity of specific reservoirs. Computer workstation technology using three-

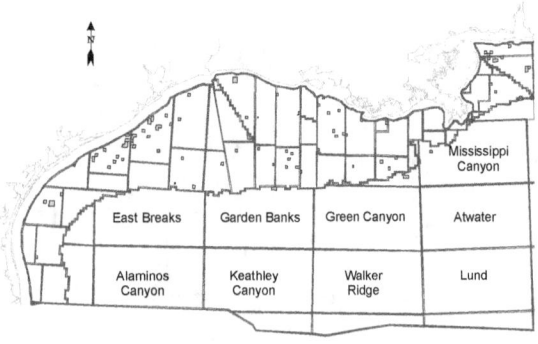

Figure 19.—Location of proved fields discovered 1990-1995, Gulf of Mexico OCS.

dimensional seismic data sets has allowed for reduced risk and greater geologic assurance in both exploration and field development. This has also allowed for exploration of new plays, such as the *Subsalt Play*. Reserve estimates for individual fields discovered in the 1990's are generally conservative and will experience significant reserves appreciation.

Figure 20 shows annual field discoveries by geologic age for the 899 proved fields. Figure 21 shows annual field discoveries of original proved reserves by geologic age for the 899 proved fields. These two figures show several trends over the last 50 years. From the mid-forties through the 1960's the largest number of fields discovered were of Miocene age and these fields contributed the largest reserves additions. This trend reflected a continuation of the

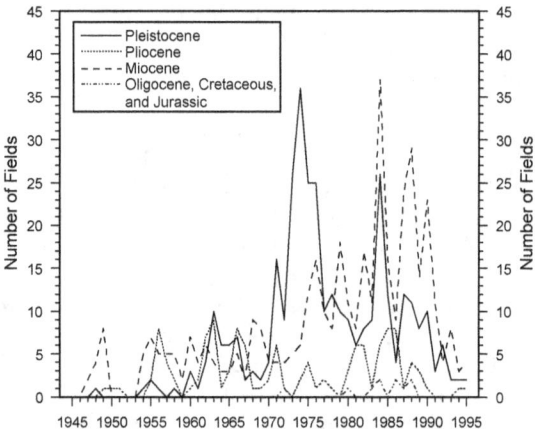

Figure 20.—Annual number of field discoveries by geologic age, 899 proved fields.

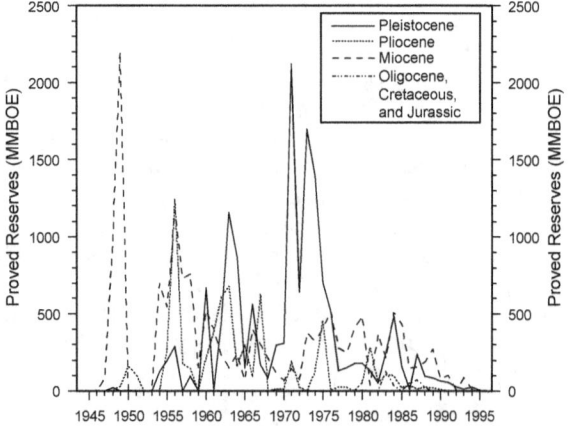

Figure 21.—Annual discoveries of original proved reserves by geologic age, 899 proved fields.

14

nearshore operating environment. The decade of the 1970's saw a large peak in discoveries of Pleistocene fields and a correspondingly large addition of Pleistocene age reserves. Technological advances in seismic data and deeper drilling accounted for the resurgence of Miocene field discoveries and reserve additions in the decade of the 1980's. This decade also saw the first Jurassic Norphlet discoveries. Completing an evaluation of the 1990's is premature, but the large discoveries in Pleistocene, Pliocene, and Miocene deepwater reservoirs will surely play a major role in future production.

Field-Size Distribution

Reserve sizes are expressed in terms of barrels of oil equivalent (BOE) and added to the liquid reserves. The conversion factor of 5,620 standard cubic feet of gas equals 1 BOE is based on the average heating values of domestic hydrocarbons. For field-size distribution ranges, a geometric progression, developed by the USGS (Drew and others, 1982), was selected (figure 22).

Class	Deposit -size range *	Class	Deposit -size range *	Class	Deposit -size range *
1	0 to 0.006	8	0.38 to 0.76	14	24.3 to 48.6
2	0.006 to 0.012	9	0.76 to 1.52	15	48.6 to 97.2
3	0.012 to 0.024	10	1.52 to 3.04	16	97.2 to 194.3
4	0.024 to 0.047	11	3.04 to 6.07	17	194.3 to 388.6
5	0.047 to 0.095	12	6.07 to 12.14	18	388.6 to 777.2
6	0.095 to 0.190	13	12.14 to 24.3	19	777.2 to 1554.4
7	0.190 to 0.380		* Million barrels of oil equivalent (MMBOE)		

Figure 22.—Description of deposit-size classes.

For field-size distribution deposit-class sizes 1 through 7 were combined. In this report, fields are classified as either oil or gas; however, some fields do produce both products, making a field type determination difficult. Generally, fields with a gas/oil ratio (GOR) less than 9,700 standard cubic feet per stock tank barrel (SCF/STB) are classified as oil.

The field-size distribution based on original proved reserves for 899 proved fields is shown in figure 23(a). Of the 899 proved oil and gas fields, there are

157 proved oil fields represented in figure 24(a) and 742 gas fields shown in figure 25(a). The Western Gulf of Mexico field-size distributions are displayed on figures 23(b), 24(b), and 25(b). Figures 23(c), 24(c), and 25(c) present the Central Gulf of Mexico field-size distributions of original proved reserves. For the first time, this report will present a distribution of unproved reserves. Figure 26(a) displays the various field-size distributions for the 76 unproved fields in the Gulf of Mexico. There are 32 unproved oil fields in figure 26(b) and 44 unproved gas fields in figure 26(c).

Analysis of the 899 proved oil and gas fields indicates that the Gulf of Mexico is currently a gas-prone basin. Figure 27 summarizes the total reserves, the median (exceeded by 50%), and the mean (arithmetic average) from the field-size distributions. This figure also provides information on the largest two field-size ranges of the proved fields. The GOR (original gas divided by original oil) of the 157 proved oil fields is 3,082 SCF/STB. The GOR of the 32 unproved oil fields is 1,811 SCF/STB. The average yield (original condensate divided by original gas) for the 742 proved gas fields is 18.9 barrels of condensate per million cubic feet (Mmcf) of gas. The average yield of the 44 unproved gas fields is 50.4 barrels of condensate per Mmcf.

Figure 28 shows the cumulative percent distribution of original proved reserves in billion barrels of oil equivalent (BBOE), by field rank. All 899 proved fields in the Gulf of Mexico OCS are included in this figure. A characteristic often observed in hydrocarbon-producing basins is a rapid dropoff in size from the largest known field to the smaller ones. Twenty-five percent of the original proved reserves are contained in the 22 largest fields. Fifty percent of the original proved reserves are contained in the 73 largest fields. Ninety percent of the original proved reserves are contained in the 346 largest fields.

Figure 29 shows the distribution of the number of fields and original proved reserves by water depth. The water depth ranges used in this figure, 651-1,300 ft, 1,301-2,600 ft, and greater than 2,600 ft, closely approximate the 200-400 meter, 400-800 meter and greater than 800 meter water depths used in the *OCS Deepwater Royalty Relief Act (DWRRA)*. Original proved reserves, reported in million barrels of oil equivalent (MMBOE), are associated with the 899 proved fields. The 76 unproved active fields are presented to show current interest and development. Sixty-nine percent of the original proved reserves in the Gulf of Mexico are located in less than 200 ft. of water.

15

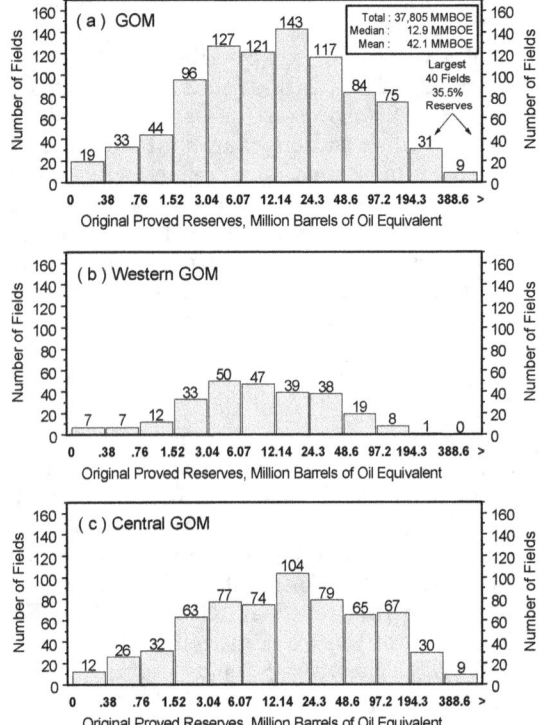

Figure 23.—Field-size distribution of proved fields. (a) 899 fields, GOM; (b) 261 fields, Western GOM; (c) 638 fields, Central GOM.

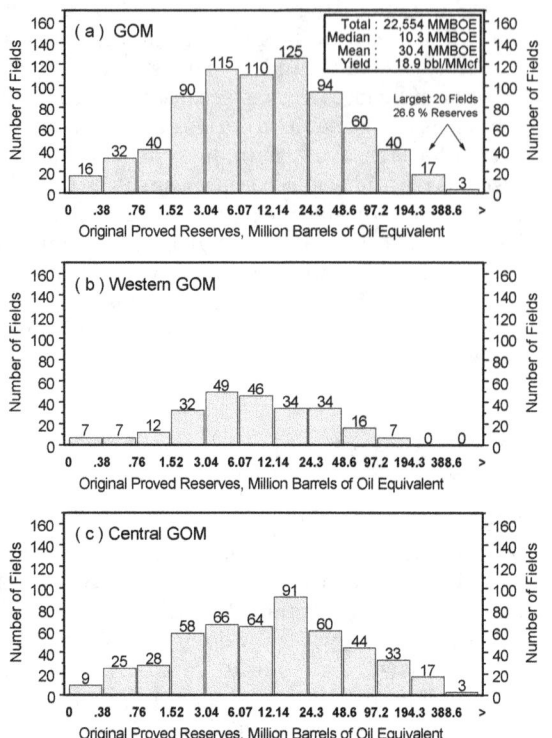

Figure 25.—Field-size distribution of proved gas fields. (a) 742 fields, GOM; (b) 244 fields, Western GOM; (c) 498 fields, Central GOM.

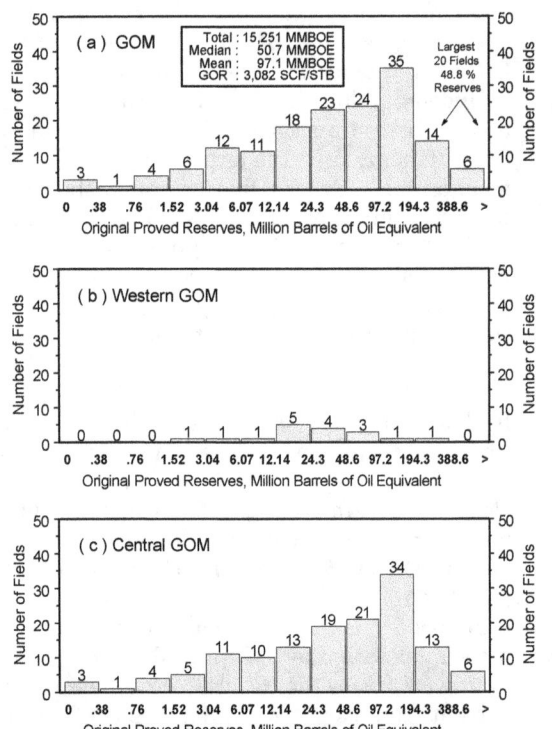

Figure 24.—Field-size distribution of proved oil fields. (a) 157 fields, GOM; (b) 17 fields, Western GOM; (c) 140 fields, Central GOM.

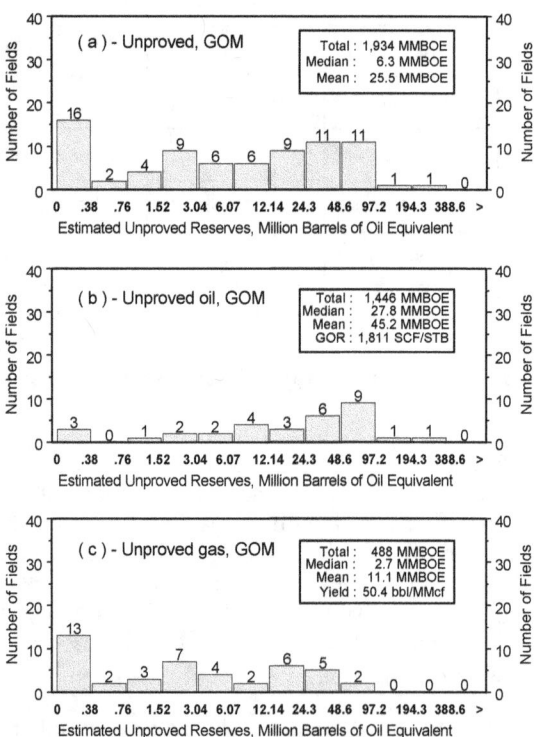

Figure 26.—Field-size distribution of unproved fields. (a) 76 fields, GOM; (b) 32 oil fields, GOM; (c) 44 gas fields, GOM.

16

Description of Fields	Figure Number	Median *	Mean *	Largest Fields	
				Number	Reserves
899 Proved	Fig. 23a	12.9	42.1	40	36 %
157 Proved Oil	Fig. 24a	50.7	97.1	20	49 %
742 Proved Gas	Fig. 25a	10.3	30.4	20	27 %
76 Unproved	Fig. 26a	6.3	25.5		
32 Unproved Oil	Fig. 26b	27.8	45.2		
44 Unproved Gas	Fig. 26c	2.7	11.1		
* Million barrels of oil equivalent (MMBOE)					

Figure 27.—GOM field-size distribution.

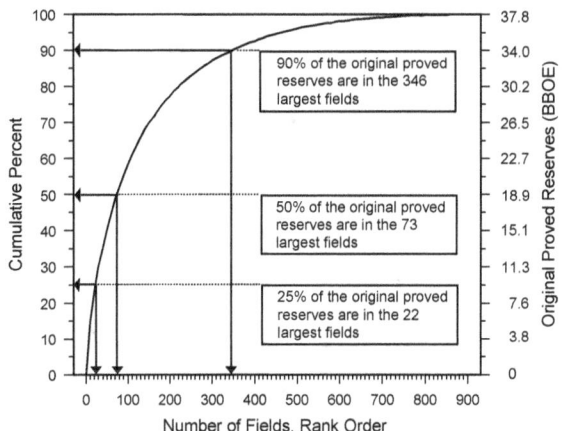

Figure 28.—Cumulative percent total reserves versus rank order of field size for 899 proved fields.

The shelf, generally considered as less than 650 ft of water, accounts for 94 percent of the original proved reserves. Development of the slope, generally considered greater than 650 ft of water, reflects a sizable amount of original proved reserves associated with a few fields. The mean original proved reserves per proved field in the Gulf of Mexico is 42.1 MMBOE. For fields in water depths between 651 and 1,300 ft, the mean original proved reserves per proved field is 50.6 MMBOE. For fields in water depths greater than 1,300 ft, the mean original proved reserves per proved field is 101.9 MMBOE. This is expected, given the economics associated with deepwater drilling and development.

Figure 30 shows the largest 20 fields based on remaining proved reserves. The top six fields lie in water depths of greater than 1,300 ft and account for 14 percent of the remaining proved reserves in the Gulf of Mexico.

Estimates of original proved reserves on the slope are increasing. This trend is expected to continue in the future due to additional exploration and development. Of the 34 proved fields in water depths greater than 650 ft, 28 are producing, 2 are depleted, and 4 are undeveloped. In 1994, MC807 (MARS) was added to the original proved reserve estimates with 166 MMBOE. In 1995, MC731 (MENSA) was added to the original proved reserves estimates with 116 MMBOE. There are 37 unproved active fields in water depths greater than 650 feet containing 1,609 MMBOE of estimated unproved reserves. This represents 83 percent of the total unproved reserves in the Gulf of Mexico.

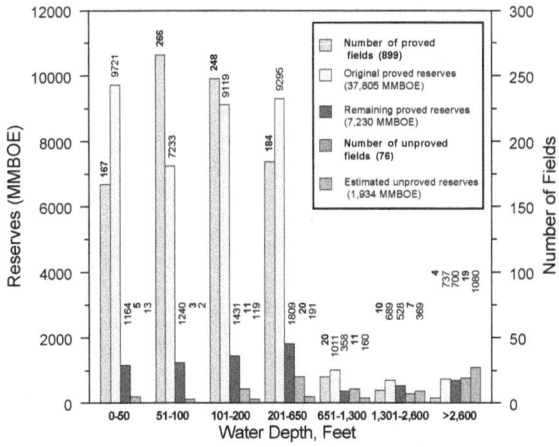

Figure 29.—Field and reserves distribution by water depth.

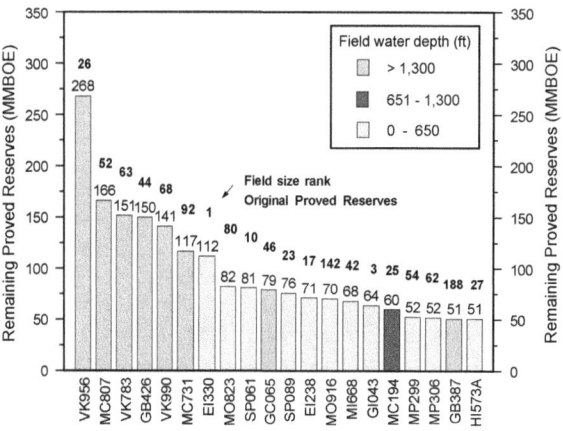

Figure 30.—Largest 20 fields based on remaining proved reserves.

Planned deepwater development in the Gulf of Mexico will likely help slow the trend of declining domestic production and rising oil imports. Exploration and development are expected to increase with technological advances, expansion of the infrastructure, and the enactment of the *OCS DWRRA*. This act gives industry the incentive to explore and produce deepwater resources.

Table 4 lists the 60 largest proved fields ranked by original proved reserves based on BOE. Rank, field name, new discoveries, discovery year, water depth, field type, field GOR, original proved reserves, cumulative production through 1995, and remaining proved reserves are presented. A complete listing of all 899 proved fields, ranked by original proved reserves, is currently available on the MMS Gulf of Mexico Region's Internet Homepage or by contacting the MMS at 1-800-200-GULF. Fields discovered in 1994 and 1995 have their names replaced with asterisks to preserve the proprietary nature of the data. Thirty new fields, proved in 1995, are identified by an asterisk in the column labeled 'New Disc'. Reserve data for unproved fields will not be listed.

Reservoir-Size Distribution

The size distributions of the proved reservoirs are shown in Figures 31, 32, and 33. The size ranges, which are based on original proved reserves, are presented on a geometrically progressing, horizontal scale. These sizes also correspond with the USGS deposit-size ranges shown in figure 22; however, for figures 32 and 33, the proved reserves are presented in MMbbl and Bcf, respectively. The number of reservoirs in each size grouping, shown as percentages of the total, is presented on a linear vertical scale. For the combination reservoirs (saturated oil rims with associated gas caps), shown in figure 31, gas is converted to BOE and added to the liquid reserves. Proved uneconomic reservoirs are excluded from these distributions, but are included in the Table 3 series.

Figure 31 shows the reservoir-size distribution, based on original proved BOE, for 1,486 proved combination reservoirs. The median is 1.1 MMBOE and the mean is 3.4 MMBOE. The GOR for the oil portion of the reservoirs is 1,522 SCF/STB, and the yield for the gas cap is 21.6 barrels of condensate per MMcf of gas.

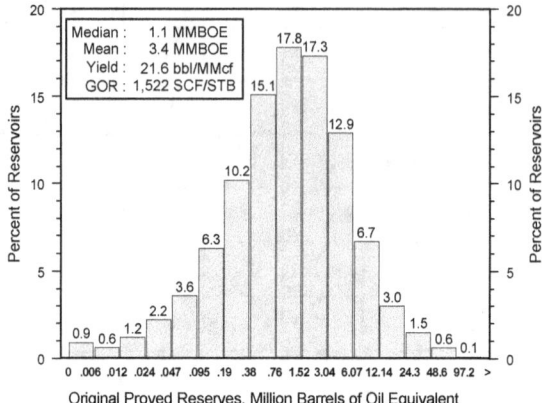

Figure 31.—Reservoir-size distribution, 1,486 proved combination reservoirs.

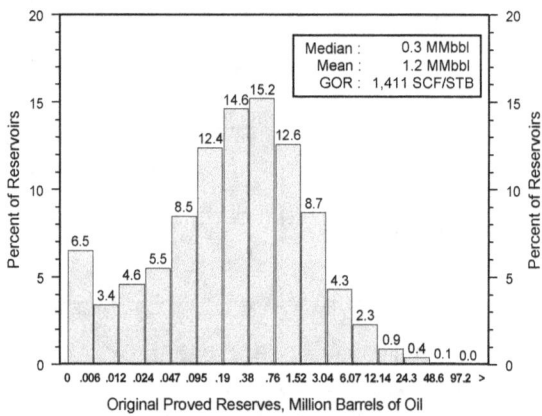

Figure 32.—Reservoir-size distribution, 6,554 proved oil reservoirs.

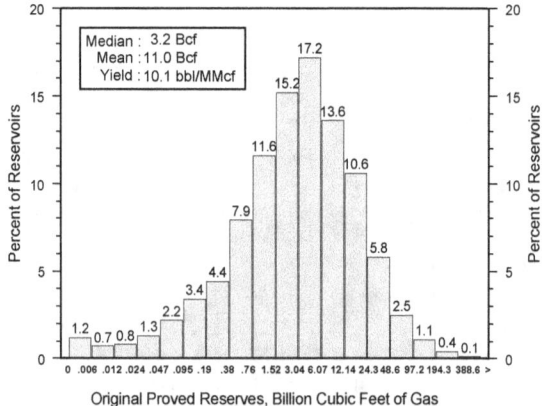

Figure 33.—Reservoir-size distribution, 11,089 proved gas reservoirs.

Table 4.—Gulf of Mexico fields by rank order, based on original proved BOE reserves, top 60 fields.

Rank	Field Name	New Disc	Disc year	Water depth	Field type	Field GOR	Original proved reserves			Cumulative production through 1995		Remaining proved reserves	
							BOE	Oil	Gas	Oil	Gas	Oil	Gas
				(feet)		(SCF/STB)	(MMbbl)	(MMbbl)	(Bcf)	(MMbbl)	(Bcf)	(MMbbl)	(Bcf)
1	EI 330		71	245	O	4463	732.3	408.1	1821.6	341.0	1570.7	67.1	251.0
2	WD 030		49	49	O	1515	668.2	526.4	797.3	502.8	735.1	23.5	62.2
3	GI 043		56	140	O	4055	633.2	367.8	1491.5	332.9	1329.9	34.9	161.6
4	TS 000		58	13	G	86617	614.3	37.4	3241.9	35.3	3002.7	2.1	239.2
5	BM 002		49	50	O	1053	614.1	517.2	544.4	488.0	481.7	29.2	62.6
6	VR 014		56	27	G	63273	599.6	48.9	3094.6	46.0	2865.5	2.9	229.1
7	MP 041		56	41	O	5580	458.4	230.0	1283.7	219.9	1190.9	10.1	92.8
8	VR 039		48	38	G	79012	457.3	30.4	2399.6	28.3	2335.9	2.1	63.6
9	SS 208		60	105	O	5744	424.8	210.1	1206.8	193.1	1134.3	17.1	72.5
10	SP 061		67	225	O	1754	359.5	274.0	480.5	211.2	379.3	62.8	101.2
11	GI 016		48	53	O	1227	355.0	291.4	357.5	281.9	343.3	9.5	14.3
12	WD 073		62	179	O	1919	339.7	253.3	486.0	230.1	423.4	23.2	62.6
13	ST 172		63	98	G	193650	317.5	9.0	1733.8	8.4	1553.0	0.6	180.9
14	EI 292		64	217	G	89154	312.2	18.5	1650.7	14.5	1462.9	4.0	187.8
15	ST 021		57	46	O	1582	310.1	242.0	382.9	229.2	356.6	12.8	26.2
16	WC 180		61	47	G	169459	298.8	9.6	1625.4	9.2	1562.4	0.4	63.0
17	EI 238		64	147	G	18770	296.7	68.4	1283.1	50.5	983.7	17.9	299.4
18	SP 027		54	63	O	5050	296.1	156.0	787.6	142.6	683.7	13.4	103.9
19	SS 176		56	100	G	21544	289.4	59.9	1289.9	55.0	1176.1	4.9	113.7
20	EC 064		57	49	G	57456	287.6	25.6	1472.1	23.5	1400.4	2.1	71.7
21	SM 048		61	100	G	52797	286.7	27.6	1456.2	23.8	1347.5	3.8	108.6
22	WD 079		66	125	O	3807	286.7	170.9	650.6	154.4	581.8	16.6	68.9
23	SP 089		69	425	O	3284	283.0	178.6	586.6	140.7	374.7	37.9	211.9
24	EI 296		71	213	G	68758	275.7	20.8	1432.5	19.8	1345.1	1.0	87.5
25	MC 194		75	1023	O	3011	274.1	178.5	537.5	151.4	353.9	27.1	183.6
26	VK 956		85	3255	O	5088	268.1	140.7	716.1	0.0	0.0	140.7	716.1
27	HI 573A		73	341	O	7962	241.5	99.9	795.6	82.5	608.9	17.4	186.6
28	ST 135		56	130	O	2851	239.9	159.2	453.8	151.8	408.6	7.3	45.2
29	EC 271		71	174	G	18694	236.4	54.6	1021.5	49.3	968.9	5.3	52.6
30	ST 176		63	128	G	12591	232.1	71.6	901.9	63.9	817.7	7.7	84.2
31	SM 130		73	215	O	1408	231.3	184.9	260.4	164.2	194.8	20.7	65.6
32	SM 066		63	125	G	242750	228.7	5.2	1256.1	4.4	1111.5	0.8	144.6
33	GI 047		55	87	O	3668	224.6	135.9	498.5	125.7	446.2	10.2	52.3
34	WC 192		54	57	G	58997	217.3	18.9	1115.2	16.7	1056.5	2.2	58.8
35	VR 076		49	31	G	192999	217.1	6.1	1185.6	4.8	1061.3	1.4	124.2
36	SM 023		60	82	G	37424	214.1	28.0	1046.2	26.3	951.4	1.7	94.8
37	SS 222		66	142	G	12450	208.4	64.8	807.1	58.1	767.6	6.8	39.5
38	SP 078		72	204	G	13115	203.4	61.0	800.3	45.4	670.2	15.6	130.0
39	WC 071		55	40	G	55505	200.2	18.4	1021.6	17.1	953.3	1.3	68.3
40	SP 062		65	331	O	1490	198.0	156.5	233.2	134.2	188.3	22.4	44.9
41	SS 113		55	41	O	3917	194.2	114.5	448.3	102.4	393.3	12.0	55.0
42	MI 668		80	95	G	352535	192.9	3.0	1067.2	1.9	692.5	1.2	374.8
43	EI 032		49	12	G	17031	190.4	47.2	804.5	39.7	780.6	7.5	23.9
44	GB 426		87	2864	O	4266	186.5	106.0	452.3	26.7	57.4	79.3	394.9
45	WC 533		73	171	G	5320619	182.3	0.2	1023.2	0.0	870.5	0.2	152.7
46	GC 065		83	1352	O	1384	180.1	144.5	200.1	80.4	117.5	64.1	82.6
47	SS 169		60	62	O	5748	177.8	87.9	505.2	81.2	460.5	6.7	44.7
48	MI 623		80	82	G	90540	172.9	10.1	915.1	7.1	656.2	3.0	258.9
49	SS 230		62	118	O	2569	171.8	117.9	302.8	106.8	257.5	11.1	45.3
50	SS 028		49	13	G	37322	169.2	22.1	826.7	19.5	740.4	2.6	86.3
51	SS 207		67	103	O	3776	167.7	100.3	378.7	96.4	338.5	3.9	40.2
52	MC 807		89	2958	O	1411	166.1	132.8	187.3	0.0	0.0	132.8	187.3
53	WC 045		49	33	G	38286	166.0	21.2	813.3	19.8	789.7	1.5	23.6
54	MP 299		62	209	O	699	165.6	147.3	102.9	102.3	62.1	45.0	40.8
55	EI 266		62	163	G	260975	162.6	3.4	894.4	2.3	798.3	1.2	96.1
56	SM 269		73	32	G	12722	162.3	49.7	632.6	43.8	500.6	5.9	132.0
57	SM 128		74	220	O	2166	162.2	117.0	253.5	106.7	218.5	10.4	35.0
58	EI 126		50	38	O	1311	159.7	129.5	169.8	121.7	155.8	7.8	13.9
59	EI 276		64	166	O	2955	159.2	104.4	308.4	92.6	276.5	11.8	32.0
60	SP 065		67	295	O	1164	158.3	131.1	152.6	117.1	109.5	14.0	43.1

A complete listing of all proved fields is available in digital format.

Figure 32 shows the reservoir-size distribution, based on original proved oil, for 6,554 proved undersaturated oil reservoirs. The median is 0.3 million barrels of oil (MMbbl), the mean is 1.2 MMbbl, and the GOR is 1,411 SCF/STB.

Figure 33 shows the reservoir-size distribution, based on original proved gas, for 11,089 proved nonassociated gas reservoirs. The median is 3.2 billion cubic feet (Bcf) of gas, the mean is 11.0 Bcf, and the yield is 10.1 barrels of condensate per MMcf of gas.

Production Rates and Discovery Trends

The mean daily production in the Gulf of Mexico OCS during 1995 was 789,000 barrels (bbl) of crude oil, 156,000 bbl of gas condensate, 1.63 Bcf of casinghead gas, and 11.45 Bcf of gas-well gas. The mean GOR of oil wells was 2,065 SCF/STB, and the mean yield from gas wells was 13.65 barrels of condensate per MMcf of gas.

Figures 34 and 35 show the frequency distribution of monthly production for completions active during 1995. Since the number of completions within a given range changes from month to month, the completion numbers presented are means of the 1995 monthly completion totals for each production range. The numbers shown in parentheses are also means of monthly counts for completions considered to be on continuous production. Completions off production for more than two days a month are not counted as continuously producing completions.

Figure 36 summarizes the data from monthly distributions of oil and gas production rates. The highest reported monthly oil production volume was from a Pliocene reservoir with a depth of 18,975 ft, during the month of July. The highest reported monthly gas production volume was from a Miocene reservoir with a subsea depth of 15,150 ft, during the month of December. The mean number of oil completions producing more than 1,000 bbl per day was 125 and the mean number of gas completions producing more than 10 MMcf per day was 276.

Annual production in the Gulf of Mexico OCS is shown in figure 37. The oil plot includes condensate, and the gas plot includes casinghead gas. Annual oil production is trimodal, reaching 376 MMbbl per year in 1971, and 350 to 356 MMbbl per year from 1984 through 1986. From 1986 through 1990 annual oil production declined 23 percent.

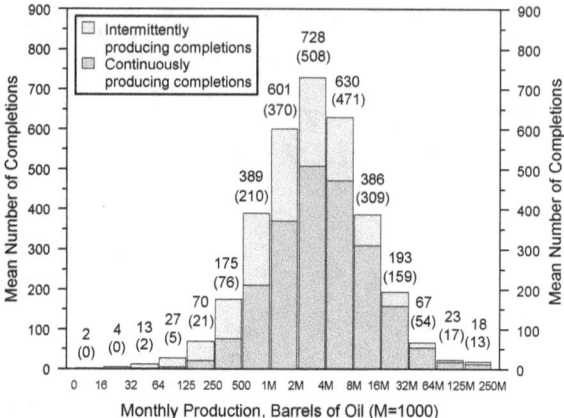

Figure 34.—Monthly distribution of oil production, 3,326 completions, (2,215) continuously producing completions.

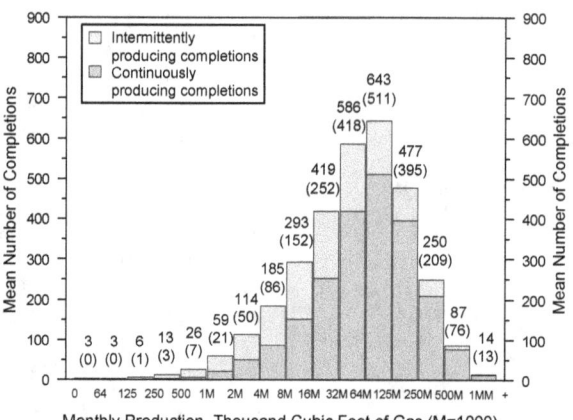

Figure 35.—Monthly distribution of gas production, 3,178 completions, (2,194) continuously producing completions.

1995	Oil	Gas
Mean Number of Producing Completions	3,326	3,178
Mean Number of Continuously Producing Completions	2,215	2,194
Highest Monthly Mean Number of Producing Completions	3,373 (April)	3,245 (January)
Lowest Monthly Mean Number of Producing Completions	3,233 (October)	3,111 (October)
Mean Production	7,210 bbl (237 bbl per day)	109 MMcf (3.6 MMcf per day)
Median Production	2,883 bbl (96 bbl per day)	56.2 MMcf (1.8 MMcf per day)
Highest Producing Rate for a Completion	351,721 bbl (11,570 bbl per day)	2,883 MMcf (94.8 MMcf per day)

Figure 36.—Monthly completion and production data.

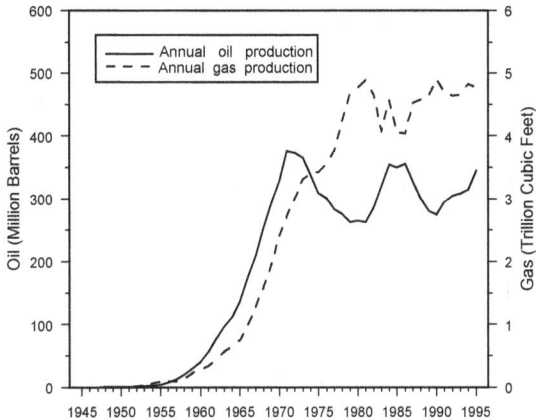

Figure 37.—Annual oil and gas production.

From 1990 through 1995 annual oil production rose from 275 MMbbl to 345 MMbbl, a 25 percent increase. Annual gas production is bimodal, reaching a peak of 4.9 Tcf per year in 1981 and 1990. From 1990 through 1993 gas production declined from 4.9 Tcf to 4.6 Tcf. The 1994 gas production of 4.8 Tcf was a 4 percent increase from 1993. Gas production decreased slightly in 1995.

Figure 38 presents original proved reserves, cumulative production, and remaining proved reserves in BBOE as of December 31, 1995, summed according to field discovery year. Field depletion may be estimated by the relative positions of the cumulative production curve and the remaining proved reserves curve. For example, if the value of the remaining proved reserves is higher than the value of cumulative production for a given year, the aggregate depletion for fields discovered that year

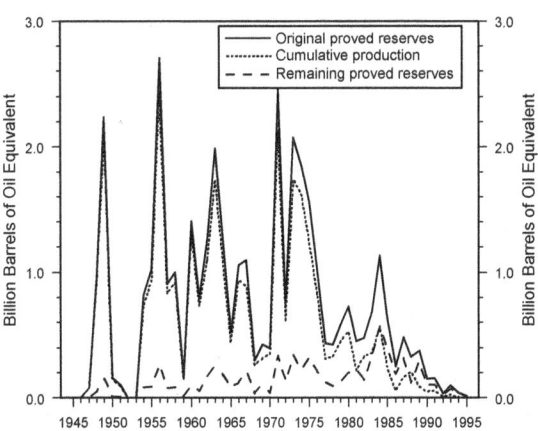

Figure 38.—Proved reserves and production by field discovery year.

is less than 50 percent. The plot demonstrates that fields discovered after 1983, with the exception of 1988, are less than 50 percent depleted. The current trend is showing that overall field sizes are decreasing.

Figure 39 is a plot of the number of proved gas and oil fields by discovery year. The annual number of gas fields discovered has been steadily increasing, while the number of oil fields discovered has not varied much from year to year, never exceeding 10 and averaging only about 3.5 discoveries per year. Through 1959, 38 percent of all fields discovered were oil. This percentage declined steadily as more gas fields were discovered until only 10 percent of the fields discovered during the 1980's were oil fields. This reflects an industry change from oil production to gas production. The shift from oil to

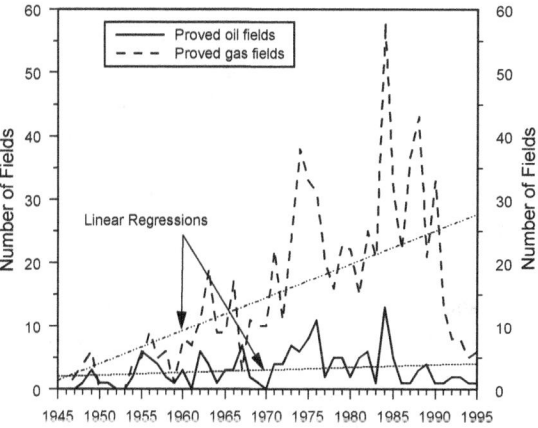

Figure 39.—Annual number of proved oil and gas field discoveries.

gas emphasis was fueled by several factors, including optimism concerning higher anticipated gas prices, realization of the inevitable decline in the size of oil fields being discovered, and the introduction of new seismic technologies that dramatically lowered the risk in identifying gas reservoirs (Lore, 1994).

Figure 40 presents the number of proved fields and the mean field size by field discovery year. This plot shows that, though the number of discovered fields has typically been increasing from year to year, the mean size of the fields has been getting smaller. The mean field size discovered for the last few years is expected to increase due to reserves growth in proved fields and reserves additions in unproved fields discovered in recent years.

21

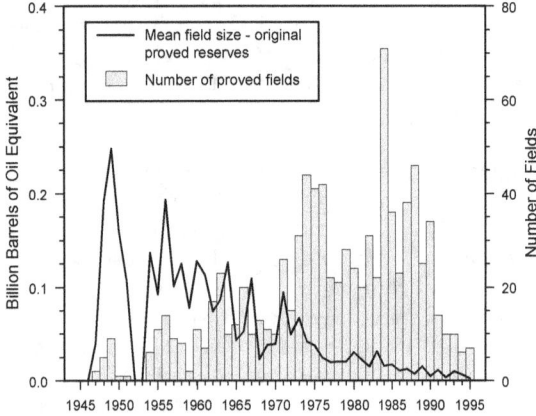

Figure 40.—Number of proved fields and mean field size by field discovery year.

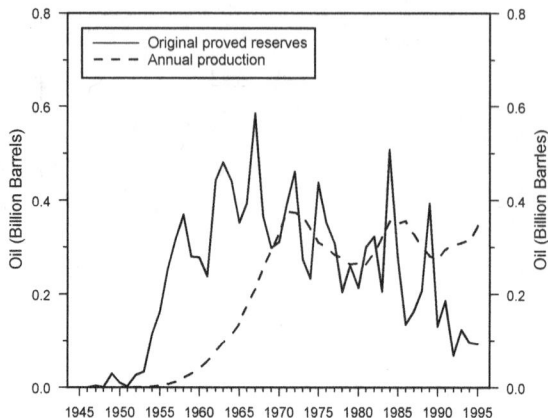

Figure 42.—Proved oil reserves by reservoir discovery year and annual oil production.

Figure 41 presents the number of proved and unproved fields and the average water depth of the fields discovered in each year. Clearly, exploration and resulting production are moving into deeper water, and this trend is expected to continue.

Figures 42 and 43 show original proved oil and gas reserves and annual production by reservoir discovery year. All data presented in figure 42 include crude oil and condensate, and all data presented in figure 43 include associated and nonassociated gas. The year of discovery assigned to a reservoir is the year in which the first well encountering hydrocarbons penetrated the reservoir. For comparison with the rate of discoveries, the annual production of oil and gas is also shown. Since 1984 new proved reservoir discoveries are no longer offsetting annual production, indicating a decreasing trend in remaining proved reserves. The original proved reserves curve in both figures is expected to increase over what is shown due to reserves growth.

Figure 44 presents the total footage drilled, the total number of wells drilled, and the number of exploratory and development wells drilled in the Gulf of Mexico OCS each year. All curves show a decline after the 1986 collapse in oil prices. A second decline occurred in 1991-92. Drilling has increased since 1992, reflecting stable energy prices and improvements in exploration and production technology.

Figure 45 presents the number of exploratory wells drilled each year by water depth. The plot shows the move toward drilling in deeper water, but also illustrates continuous drilling on the shelf.

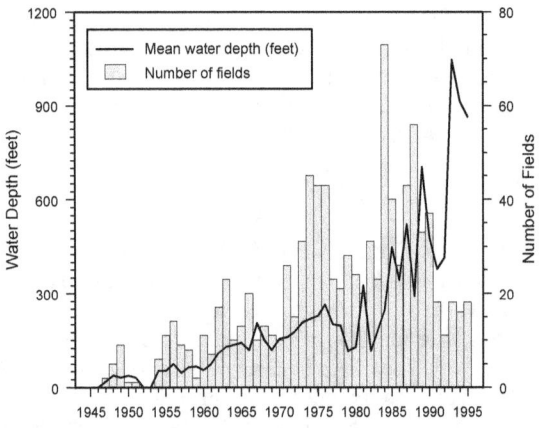

Figure 41.—Number of fields and mean water depth by field discovery year.

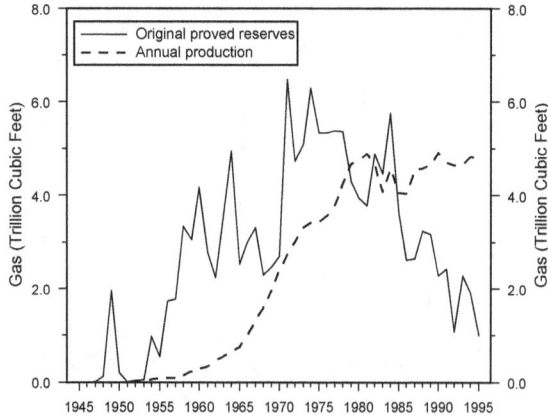

Figure 43.—Proved gas reserves by reservoir discovery year and annual gas production.

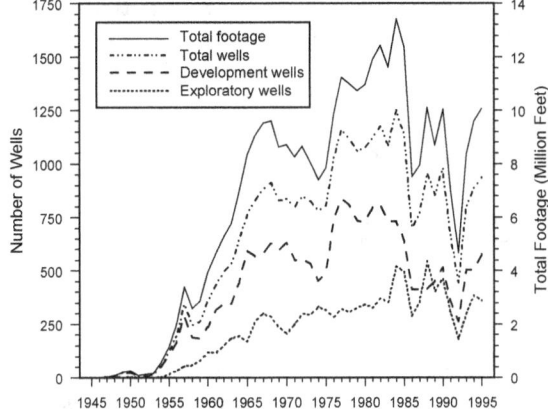

Figure 44.—Wells and footage drilled.

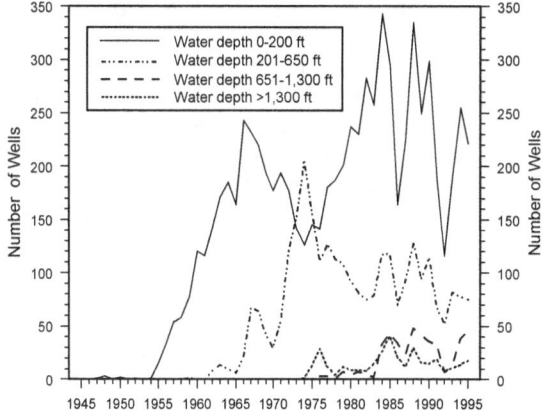

Figure 45.—Number of exploratory wells drilled by water depth.

Summary and Comparison of Proved Reserves

A summary of proved reserve estimates during the year and a comparison with estimates from last year's report (December 31, 1994) are shown in table 5. Recent proved field discoveries (4 oil fields and 26 gas fields) are summarized and tabulated as increases to original proved reserves. For further

clarification, recent proved field discoveries are identified as new fields added in the last year, even though some were discovered before 1995. Proved reserve estimates are revised as needed, resulting in increases as additional wells are drilled and new leases are added to existing fields, and decreases as reservoirs are depleted and leases relinquished. Complete reevaluations of existing field studies are conducted based upon changes in field development

Table 5.—Summary and comparison of proved oil and gas reserves as of December 31, 1994, and December 31, 1995.

	Oil (billion bbl)		Gas (trillion cu ft)	
Original proved reserves:				
Previous estimates, as of 12/31/94*	11.86		141.9	
Discoveries	+0.04		+1.4	
Revisions	+0.11		+1.6	
Adjustments	0.00		0.0	
Net change	+0.15		+3.0	
Estimate, as of 12/31/95 (this report)		12.01		144.9
Cumulative production:				
Previous estimates, as of 12/31/94*	9.34		112.6	
Adjustments	0.00		0.0	
Production during 1995	+0.34		+4.8	
Net change	+0.34		+4.8	
Estimate, as of 12/31/95 (this report)		9.68		117.4
Remaining proved reserves:				
Previous estimates, as of 12/31/94*	2.52		29.3	
Discoveries	+0.04		+1.4	
Revisions	+0.11		+1.6	
Adjustments	0.00		0.0	
Production during 1995	-0.34		-4.8	
Net change	-0.19		-1.8	
Estimate, as of 12/31/95 (this report)		2.33		27.5

*Melancon and others, 1995

23

and/or production history. Increases and decreases of proved reserves are summarized and presented as changes due to revisions. Based on periodic reviews and revisions of field studies conducted since the 1994 report, the revisions for original proved oil and gas reserves have resulted in a net increase. A net change in the original proved oil and gas reserves is a result of combining both the discoveries and the revisions.

Table 5 demonstrates that the 1995 proved oil and gas discoveries, adjustments, and field revisions did not exceed production. The remaining proved oil and gas reserves have decreased since 1994.

Table 6 presents all previous reserve estimates by year. Due to continuous adjustments and corrections to production data submitted by Gulf of Mexico OCS operators, the difference between historical cumulative production for successive years does not always equal the annual production for the latter year. No comparisons will be made for unproved reserves.

Conclusions

The 899 proved oil and gas fields in the federally regulated part of the Gulf of Mexico OCS contained original proved reserves estimated to be 12.01 billion barrels of oil and 144.9 trillion cubic feet of gas. Remaining proved reserves, as of December 31, 1995, are estimated to be 2.33 billion barrels of oil and 27.5 trillion cubic feet of gas. Estimated remaining proved oil reserves have decreased 7.5 percent and estimated remaining proved gas reserves have decreased 6.1 percent from last year's report.

The 76 unproved oil and gas fields in the federally regulated part of the Gulf of Mexico OCS contained unproved reserves estimated to be 1.20 billion barrels of oil and 4.1 trillion cubic feet of gas. Included in these estimates are unproved reserves of 1.05 billion barrels of oil and 2.2 trillion cubic feet of gas from 27 fields in water depths greater than 1,000 feet. Estimated unproved oil reserves are 3.5 times annual oil production, and estimated unproved gas reserves represent 85 percent of annual gas production. Estimated remaining proved oil reserves are expected to increase in future years due to significant moves of unproved reserves into the proved category.

Contributing Personnel

This report includes contributions from the following Gulf of Mexico Region, Office of Resource Evaluation, personnel.

David Absher	Beth Pastor
Eric Batchelder	Bruce Perry
Scott Edwards	Robert Peterson
Eric Kazanis	Katherine Ross
Theresa Keller	Christopher Schoennagel
Mike Lafleur	Chee Yu

Table 6.—Proved oil and gas reserves and cumulative production at end of year, Gulf of Mexico, Outer Continental Shelf and Slope.

Oil expressed in billions of barrels; gas in trillions of cubic feet. "Oil" includes crude oil and condensate; "gas" includes associated and nonassociated gas. Remaining proved reserves estimated as of December 31 each year.

Year	Number of fields included	Original proved reserves		Historical cumulative production		Remaining proved reserves	
		Oil	Gas	Oil	Gas	Oil	Gas
1975	255	6.61	59.9	3.82	27.2	2.79	32.7
1976	306	6.86	65.5	4.12	30.8	2.74	34.7
1977	334	7.18	69.2	4.47	35.0	2.71	34.2
1978	385	7.52	76.2	4.76	39.0	2.76	37.2
1979*	417	7.71	82.2	4.83	44.2	2.88	38.0
1980	435	8.04	88.9	4.99	48.7	3.05	40.2
1981	461	8.17	93.4	5.27	53.6	2.90	39.8
1982	484	8.56	98.1	5.58	58.3	2.98	39.8
1983	521	9.31	106.2	5.90	62.5	3.41	43.7
1984	551	9.91	111.6	6.24	67.1	3.67	44.5
1985	575	10.63	116.7	6.58	71.1	4.05	45.6
1986	645	10.81	121.0	6.93	75.2	3.88	45.8
1987	704	10.76	122.1	7.26	79.7	3.50	42.4
1988†	678	10.95	126.7	7.56	84.3	3.39	42.4
1989	739	10.87	129.1	7.84	88.9	3.03	40.2
1990	782	10.64	129.9	8.11	93.8	2.53	36.1
1991	819	10.74	130.5	8.41	98.5	2.33	32.0
1992	835	11.08	132.7	8.71	103.2	2.37	29.5
1993	849	11.15	136.8	9.01	107.7	2.14	29.1
1994	876	11.86	141.9	9.34	112.6	2.52	29.3
1995	899	12.01	144.9	9.68	117.4	2.33	27.5

*Gas plant liquids dropped from reporting system.
†Basis of reserves changed from API demonstrated to SPE proved.

References

Arps, J. J., A. F. Van Everdingen, R. W. Buchwald, and A. E. Smith, 1967, *A Statistical study of recovery efficiency*, American Petroleum Institute, Bulletin D14, p. 33.

Drew, L. J., J. H. Schuenemeyer, and W. J. Bawiec, 1982, *Estimation of the future rates of oil and gas discoveries in the western Gulf of Mexico*, Geological Survey Professional Paper 1252, United States Government Printing Office, Washington, D.C., p. 7.

Grab, F.A., and G.L. Smith, 1987, "Estimation of oil and gas reserves" (chapter 40), In: Howard B. Bradley (ed.), *Petroleum engineering handbook*, Houston, Texas, Society of Petroleum Engineers, pp. 40-1-40-38.

Lore, G.L. 1994, An Exploration and discovery model; an historic perspective—Gulf of Mexico Outer Continental Shelf, In: K. Simakov and D. Thurston (eds.), *Proceedings of the 1994 International Conference on Arctic Margins*, Russian Academy of Sciences, Magadan, p. 306-313.

Lore, G.L., J.P. Brooke, D.W. Cooke, R.J. Klazynski, D.L. Olson, and K.M. Ross, 1996, *Summary of the 1995 assessment of conventionally recoverable hydrocarbon resources of the Gulf of Mexico and Atlantic Outer Continental Shelf*, U.S. Department of the Interior, Minerals Management Service, Gulf of Mexico OCS Region, Office of Resource Evaluation, OCS Report MMS 96-0047, New Orleans, 41 p.

Melancon, J. M., S. M. Bacigalupi, C. J. Kinler, D. A. Marin, and M. T. Prendergast, 1995, *Estimated proved oil and gas reserves, Gulf of Mexico Outer Continental Shelf, December 31, 1994*: U.S. Department of the Interior, Minerals Management Service, Gulf of Mexico Region, OCS Report MMS 95-0050, New Orleans, 56 p.

Office the Federal Register, National Archives and Records Administration, 1992, *Code of Federal Regulations, 30 CFR, Mineral resources*, U.S. Government Printing Office, Washington, D.C.

Society of Petroleum Engineers (SPE) and The World Petroleum Congress (WPC) Draft Reserves Definitions, 1996, "Definitions for oil and gas reserves," *Journal of Petroleum Technology*, August 1996, p. 694-696.

U.S. Department of Energy (DOE), 1989, Conversion Factors, *Monthly Energy*, December 1989, p. 132-3. Calculated from Tables A3 and A5.

U.S. Department of the Interior, Geological Survey and Minerals Management Service, 1989, *Estimates of undiscovered conventional oil and gas resources in the United States—A Part of the Nation's energy endowment*, 44 p.

Notice

The Estimated Proved Oil and Gas Reserves Report for the Gulf of Mexico has undergone numerous changes over the last few years. We are continually striving to provide meaningful information to the users of this document. Suggested changes, additions, or deletions to our data or statistical presentations are encouraged so we can publish the most useful report possible. Please contact the Reserves Section Chief Courtney Reed at (504) 736-2950 at Minerals Management Service, 1201 Elmwood Park Boulevard, MS 5130, New Orleans, Louisiana 70123-2394, to communicate your ideas for consideration in our next report.

For free publication and digital data, visit the MMS Gulf of Mexico Internet Homepage at http://www.mms.gov/omm/gomr/.

For information on purchasing hard copies of this publication or digital data from the report contact:

Minerals Management Service
Gulf of Mexico OCS Region
Attn: Public Information Unit (MS 5034)
1201 Elmwood Park Boulevard
New Orleans, Louisiana 70123-2394
(504) 736-2519 or 1-800-200-GULF
http://www.mms.gov/omm/gomr/

Gary L. Lore
Regional Supervisor
Resource Evaluation

The Department of the Interior Mission

As the Nation's principal conservation agency, the Department of the Interior has responsibility for most of our nationally owned public lands and natural resources. This includes fostering sound use of our land and water resources; protecting our fish, wildlife, and biological diversity; preserving the environmental and cultural values of our national parks and historical places;
and providing for the enjoyment of life through outdoor recreation. The Department assesses our energy and mineral resources and works to ensure that their development is in the best interests of all our people by encouraging stewardship and citizen participation in their care. The Department also has a major responsibility for American Indian reservation communities and for people who live in island territories under U.S. administration.

The Minerals Management Service Mission

As a bureau of the Department of the Interior, the Minerals Management Service's (MMS) primary responsibilities are to manage the mineral resources located on the Nation's Outer Continental Shelf (OCS), collect revenue from the Federal OCS and onshore Federal and Indian lands, and distribute those revenues.

Moreover, in working to meet its responsibilities, the **Offshore Minerals Management Program** administers the OCS competitive leasing program and oversees the safe and environmentally sound exploration and production of our Nation's offshore natural gas, oil and other mineral resources. The MMS **Royalty Management Program** meets its responsibilities by ensuring the efficient, timely and accurate collection and disbursement of revenue from mineral leasing and production due to Indian tribes and allottee, States and the U.S. Treasury.

The MMS strives to fulfill its responsibilities through the general guiding principles of: (1) being responsive to the public's concerns and interests by maintaining a dialogue with all potentially affected parties and (2) carrying out its programs with an emphasis on working to enhance the quality of life for all Americans by lending MMS assistance and expertise to economic development and environmental protection.